THE EVERYTHING

NEW TEACHER BOOK

2ND EDITION

WITHDRAWN

Dear Reader,

You are about to embark on a grand adventure: teaching. Sometimes teaching can be an awesome experience, other times it can be extremely challenging. However, in the end it is worth it when you look at your students and see them learning, participating, and growing. I have written this book directly from my and my husband's classroom experiences, as well as those of many other teachers with whom I have worked. I hope you will find that these pages hold lessons they didn't teach you in the college of education. The information here is from the trenches. It is not based on theories of education, but rather on experience. I do hope that you enjoy this book and, more importantly, that you find true happiness and fulfillment in your profession as a teacher. You have chosen a truly amazing career. As George Bernard Shaw said, "To me the sole hope of human salvation lies in teaching."

Melissa Kelly

Welcome to the EVERYTHING® Series!

These handy, accessible books give you all you need to tackle a difficult project, gain a new hobby, comprehend a fascinating topic, prepare for an exam, or even brush up on something you learned back in school but have since forgotten.

You can choose to read an *Everything®* book from cover to cover or just pick out the information you want from our four useful boxes: e-questions, e-facts, e-alerts, and e-ssentials.

We give you everything you need to know on the subject, but throw in a lot of fun stuff along the way, too.

We now have more than 400 *Everything®* books in print, spanning such wide-ranging categories as weddings, pregnancy, cooking, music instruction, foreign language, crafts, pets, New Age, and so much more. When you're done reading them all, you can finally say you know *Everything®*!

QUESTION

Answers to
common questions

FACT

Important snippets
of information

ALERT

Urgent
warnings

ESSENTIAL

Quick
handy tips

PUBLISHER Karen Cooper

DIRECTOR OF ACQUISITIONS AND INNOVATION Paula Munier

MANAGING EDITOR, EVERYTHING® SERIES Lisa Laing

COPY CHIEF Casey Ebert

ACQUISITIONS EDITOR Lisa Laing

SENIOR DEVELOPMENT EDITOR Brett Palana-Shanahan

EDITORIAL ASSISTANT Hillary Thompson

EVERYTHING® SERIES COVER DESIGNER Erin Alexander

LAYOUT DESIGNERS Colleen Cunningham, Elisabeth Lariviere, Ashley Vierra, Denise Wallace

Visit the entire Everything® series at *www.everything.com*

THE EVERYTHING®
NEW TEACHER BOOK
2ND EDITION WITH CD

A survival guide for
the first year and beyond

Melissa Kelly, MEd

Avon, Massachusetts

To my true joys in life: Marty, Ty, and Jessalyn.

An Everything® Series Book.
Everything® and everything.com® are registered trademarks of F+W Media, Inc.

Published by Adams Media, a division of F+W Media, Inc.
57 Littlefield Street, Avon, MA 02322 U.S.A.
www.adamsmedia.com

ISBN 10: 1-4405-0038-X
ISBN 13: 978-1-4405-0038-1

Printed in the United States of America.

10 9 8 7 6 5 4 3 2 1

Library of Congress Cataloging-in-Publication Data
is available from the publisher.

This publication is designed to provide accurate and authoritative information with regard to the subject matter covered. It is sold with the understanding that the publisher is not engaged in rendering legal, accounting, or other professional advice. If legal advice or other expert assistance is required, the services of a competent professional person should be sought.

—From a *Declaration of Principles* jointly adopted by a Committee of the American Bar Association and a Committee of Publishers and Associations

Many of the designations used by manufacturers and sellers to distinguish their products are claimed as trademarks. Where those designations appear in this book and Adams Media was aware of a trademark claim, the designations have been printed with initial capital letters.

This book is available at quantity discounts for bulk purchases.
For information, please call 1-800-289-0963.

Contents

Acknowledgments

Many thanks go to the staff at Florida Virtual School, especially Julie Young and Pam Birtolo. I would also like to thank Mike Daecher from About. com, Rita Kienle, Lynn Roll, Mickey Colen, Loretta Schultz, Tom Fleming, Tim Newman, Laurie Peterson, Jennifer Smith, Lana Howe, Pat Naylor, the Ericksons, and Tammy Rabon. Without each of your special gifts, I would not have had the role models necessary to write this book. Finally, very special thanks go to my agent, Barb Doyen, for starting me out on this path, to my entire family, especially my parents who were and are my greatest teachers, to my awesome husband Marty without whom this book would not have been written, to my beautiful and amazing children Ty and Jessalyn for love and laughter through it all, and most importantly to Jesus Christ, my Lord and savior.

Top Ten Things Every New Teacher Should Know

1. Always have high (but not impossible) expectations for yourself and your students.

2. Effective classroom management starts on the first day.

3. Humor can help diffuse a tense classroom situation.

4. Consistency and fairness go hand in hand and should be practiced every day.

5. Be flexible, but don't become a doormat.

6. Smile at your students.

7. Avoid confrontations in front of other students.

8. Be friendly, but avoid becoming friends with your students.

9. Get to know the people around you, and choose your friends and battles wisely.

10. Never advertise your inexperience.

Introduction

TEACHING HAS A LONG and noble history. From the ancients, like Plato and Aristotle, to the educators of today, teachers have made a huge impact on the world around them. Almost everyone remembers one or more teachers fondly, and some people credit a particular teacher with their success in life. Teachers are hugely influential, many times in a positive way but sometimes in a negative way, too. Teachers can inspire their students to greatness—or they can inadvertently give inaccurate information that will stick with their students for a lifetime.

Being a teacher is a special calling. It takes a kind yet firm heart. It also takes a person who basically believes in the goodness of all people. A cynical teacher can cause a borderline student to lose faith and give up. On the other hand, a positive and perceptive teacher can help a student turn her life around and begin to meet her potential. Just having a positive attitude is not enough, though. A classroom teacher relies on many special skills.

Lee Iacocca said, "In a completely rational society, the best of us would aspire to be teachers and the rest of us would have to settle for something less, because passing civilization along from one generation to the next ought to be the highest honor and the highest responsibility anyone could have." Teaching can be a stressful and sometimes a thankless job, but when a teacher finally does see that he is making a difference, he receives a reward like no other.

As a new teacher, you will be faced with many challenges and, hopefully, will reap many rewards. *The Everything® New Teacher Book, 2nd Edition with CD* is designed to be a tool that can help guide you down the path of effectiveness, leading to the ultimate goal of a truly rewarding career. Though it is designed for the novice, more experienced teachers will also find it useful in their day-to-day careers.

Teaching is truly a cumulative activity. The advice in this book is drawn from the accumulated experience of many teachers. You can trust that the information you find here is based on what really happens in the classroom. It is not "pie in the sky" theory but realistic and effective practice. Most of the information in this book can be used from day one. In fact, much of it should be implemented *before* the first day of classes.

One of the main reasons that new teachers have such a tough time in the beginning is that they do not feel comfortable in their position. Because of their lack of experience, they make some very common mistakes, like making friends with students or being lax in terms of discipline. In fact, most new teachers start to worry about keeping discipline before they even enter the field. It is one of the more difficult challenges that a new teacher faces. This book aims to steer you around those common errors and keep you from making them in the first place.

As a new teacher, you will be in survival mode for the first few weeks of school. However, after things calm down and you begin to feel comfortable in front of your students, you may begin looking beyond the latest house-keeping task to the big picture, which includes the school at large. As with any new career, you will be faced with a new vocabulary and customs. The school culture is like no other industry because of the unique nature of its "product": educated children. This book is designed to give you some insight into the inner workings of the school system. You will learn about the trends and ideas that abound in education today. Just knowing what these terms and ideas mean can help you converse intelligently with your coworkers and administration.

Not every person is cut out to teach. However, if you feel the calling and you work to improve yourself, you can be an effective teacher, the kind of teacher who truly makes a difference in her students' lives. As Henry Adams said, "A teacher affects eternity; he can never tell where his influence stops."

CHAPTER 1

Welcome to Teaching

Effective teaching is both a science and an art. Formal education can lay the foundation through the examination of various theories of effective teaching, but nothing can replace the experience of being out in the trenches. The art of teaching comes mainly from observation and experience. The scenarios and examples in this book are drawn from real life to help prepare you for your teaching career. The first step to becoming an effective teacher is to have a clear picture of what teaching is really like.

The Noble Profession

Consider why you became a teacher. What made you decide to devote your life's work to teaching? Was it an influential teacher you admired, a desire to help others, or some other personal reason? At times, teaching can be a thankless profession, so you need to find your satisfaction from within. Yes, you will receive some rewards, but from day to day, you will have to create your own support system.

The teaching profession is a true calling. Not everyone is cut out to be a teacher. Some people just don't have the patience. Others are not detail-oriented enough to keep up with the logistics and paperwork. Inflexible people will find that they have a hard time working within the strictures of a school system. If you are in teaching for the money, you will probably be disappointed. However, if you approach teaching as a calling and a noble endeavor, you will find satisfaction.

Education Today

Education is in a state of flux. It's commonly believed, whether accurately or not, that something is seriously wrong with education in the United States. Politicians often run on education-reform platforms. Reform is also a common topic on talk shows and news reports.

Changing Attitudes about Education

The truth is that no one has a real handle on the issues and problems with education in America today. The reasons are multifaceted and deal with the core of our changing society itself:

- Attitudes among parents have changed. Many parents no longer choose to be partners in their children's discipline process.
- The teacher's role has expanded but is no longer well defined, so many teachers lose their focus.
- It's difficult to remove ineffective teachers from the school system.
- Society has become more permissive as a whole. Less emphasis is placed on personal responsibility.

- Student attitudes have changed over time. A greater number of students today believe that teachers and schools must accept them the way they are.
- Administration is often stymied by laws and budget concerns. It no longer joins teachers to create a consistent message and outlook on education.

It is obvious that because of all of these intersecting and conflicting issues, the ideas on how to "fix" education are varied. Educational professionals, parent groups, politicians, editorialists, and many others have their own opinions on which reforms are necessary to overcome these difficulties. However, the task is extremely difficult, if not impossible, because the solutions have to alter people's attitudes and actions.

ALERT

It is often difficult to adjust to the newest educational reforms. Changing the structure of your teaching day or year can be disruptive, both to you and to your students. Keep a positive attitude, and realize that reforms come and go, but the things that make you an effective teacher will never change.

The Changing World of Reform

Many of the proposed reforms don't provide solutions. They merely offer a bandage for the battered system of education. This does not mean, however, that education in America is dying or already dead. It is alive and well in the classroom of every effective teacher.

Education reforms are like swings of a pendulum. If you have been in education long enough, reforms that you thought were long forgotten will be revived, dusted off, and given a new coat of paint. As a teacher, you should be prepared to see your school jump on the reform bandwagon at some point. While many reform movements have good points, adopting them can cause problems. School systems often invest a lot of time, effort, and money into a specific reform. With all this investment, it can be hard for schools to admit if a reform does not work as planned.

Reforms will happen to your school sooner or later, so you may expect any of the following:

- Year-round education
- Block scheduling
- 4 × 4 scheduling
- High-stakes testing
- Learning communities
- School voucher system

Each of these reforms has its champions and its critics. They all will be discussed in greater depth in Chapter 20.

Your Role as a Teacher

The role of teachers has expanded to a point that it will sometimes be difficult for you to grasp exactly what is expected of you. Today, education is the topic of many social and political debates. The problems that education faces are not clear-cut, and the answers to these problems are even less apparent. In this atmosphere of blame and reform, teachers often find themselves sinking instead of soaring. To keep your sanity, you must define the role you are going to have in education.

Teaching has become much more complicated over time. Teachers wear many hats:

- Facilitator
- Coach
- Nurse
- Knowledge specialist
- Special-education expert
- Surrogate parent
- Record keeper
- Guidance counselor
- Technology expert
- Social worker

The truth is that no one person can fulfill all of these roles. It is your job as a teacher to decide where to put your emphasis. Develop a clear vision of the role you want to play. This will give you the power to make a much greater impact and will also shield you from the pressures and stresses that affect many other teachers.

Choosing Your Roles

So how do you decide where to place your emphasis? One way to begin is to rank the roles in order of importance according to your beliefs. It is an interesting exercise to create a similar list according to how you believe your school would rank these roles. Compare the two lists. If you are feeling frustrated, it may be that your values are conflicting.

To be a successful and happy teacher, it is advisable to work in a setting that matches your values as closely as possible. However, it may not be possible to quit your position at a school where your values conflict. Just having a clearer picture of why you are experiencing difficulties in this kind of situation can help you find ways to cope.

Administrators, colleagues, parents, and students will pull you in many different directions. Have a strong foundation for what you believe your role should be, and you will be better armed to meet the challenges you face.

A Day in the Life of a Teacher

It is important to remember that no one is born with the skills, understanding, and experience to be an effective teacher. However, with perseverance, a positive attitude, and the tools found in this book, you can be successful. Teaching may be challenging, surprising, and even exciting. Days are often filled with unexpected events and are also occasionally blessed by amazing rewards. These, of course, are what make teaching worthwhile. One thing is certain: Rarely is any day in the life of a teacher "typical."

The Basic Schedule

As a teacher, you usually get to school early and leave late. Your day probably begins with some planning time that allows you to make last-minute preparations for the students. Once the students arrive in the classroom, you will probably not get another moment of quiet until your next planning period or the end of the day. In fact, some elementary teachers do not get a planning period each day of the week. In such cases, they might only get planning time when their students leave for their enrichment activities such as art and physical education.

Each class is a new challenge. You will find some students who love learning and some who despise it. You will present your lesson and may not have any unexpected disruptions. When the day ends, you will probably have meetings to attend before you can settle down to grading and planning for the next day.

ALERT

Sometimes new teachers don't get the same consideration as those who have worked at a school for a while. If you feel that you are not being treated fairly by colleagues or the office staff and administration, find a mentor at your school who can help you work through these issues.

Unexpected Events

Part of the challenge of teaching is dealing with the many unexpected events that will arise each day. Here are just some examples of these events:

- **Office announcements:** While schools try to limit these during class time, it may still happen a few times each week.
- **Fire drills:** Most fire drills are announced beforehand, but there may be times that a student pulls the alarm as a prank.
- **Minor student disruptions:** Minor disruptions, such as inappropriate talking, happen on a daily basis.
- **Major student disruptions:** Everybody hopes to avoid major disruptions, but they still happen—to all teachers.
- **Unexpected visitors:** Students on official or unofficial business, other teachers or administrators, and even parents have been known to unexpectedly interrupt class time.

- **Unannounced assemblies:** While most assemblies are announced beforehand, sometimes you will be given only a day's or even a few hours' notice.
- **Guidance interruptions:** In high schools at certain times of the year, it is common for guidance counselors to call students to meetings and appointments.
- **Other disruptions:** Many other disruptions will arise when least expected, including unlikely events like very noisy construction work or power outages.

As this list shows, it is in your best interest to be flexible and expect the unexpected. Be ready to change your lesson plans at a moment's notice. And always remember to keep your sense of humor.

A Teacher's Rewards

Some days will also be filled with rewards. While you should not expect these little treats, you can feel confident that they will happen. A chronically disruptive student might experience a turnaround, a slower student might grasp a difficult concept, or a simple discussion might serve as an excellent educational experience. These are the moments that will continue to motivate you through your career.

ESSENTIAL

It is useful to keep a journal with positive observations, clippings, and student comments throughout your teaching career. When you are feeling stressed or burned out, just pull out your journal and get recharged.

One of the most wonderful rewards of teaching is having former students come back to tell you how much you influenced them. Students will sometimes write you letters or notes expressing how important you were or are to them. If you remember back to your school days, you can probably think of a couple of teachers who were truly influential. Strive to be that teacher for your students, and you will be well rewarded.

What Your Students Expect from You

A week or two before school starts, students start gearing up for the new year. They usually get their new class schedules in the mail or go to their school for a meet-the-teacher event. They've probably been shopping for new school clothes and supplies. When the first day arrives, most will come prepared with clean notebooks, fresh boxes of crayons, and unsharpened pencils.

Something else happens at this same time: Students get excited. Many, if not most, students come back to school with a new attitude and with definite expectations of doing well. As a teacher, you will also find that the start of the school year is an exciting time. You will have the opportunity to get to know a whole new group of students and to teach them important information and life skills.

Students Want to Succeed

All people want to succeed, even if they fear success. Many students realize that they could have done a better job in their last school year. The new school year is the perfect time to turn over a new leaf and start fresh.

With this in mind, students often approach the first school day the same way that many people approach the new year. While they might not consciously write down a list of resolutions, they have them all the same. As a teacher, your challenge will be to see how long you can keep this excitement brewing. This is not to say that you can ever hope to replace video games or television, but there are ways to make your classroom environment fun and engaging.

Students Are as Nervous as You

Remember the last time you were put in a new classroom with a teacher you had never met? Even if you had a friend or two in the class, there was probably an element of nervousness in the air. Many of your students will feel the same. Fear of the unknown is a normal part of human nature. You and your class are unknown elements to the students before they arrive on that first day.

Students will show their nervousness in a variety of ways. Most of them will probably be very quiet. Even if you try to make a joke, you might not get a lot of response. It will take some coaxing to get students out of their shells. Learning students' names quickly can help them feel more welcome and relaxed.

FACT

While students might feel nervous on the first day, this nervousness will quickly disappear if you make them feel safe, welcome, and engaged. Remember, you set the tone for your class.

A couple of students might come into your class on the first day with a chip on their shoulders. This too is a sign of nervousness. These students don't feel comfortable, so they become defensive. Just knowing this can help you make better decisions on how to react to a student's misbehavior. This does not mean that this attitude is acceptable, but it is not necessarily an indication of future behavioral problems. While behavior management will be covered in great detail in Chapter 5, know that the biggest tool you have in your arsenal at this point is your sense of humor.

Students Wait to See How You Act

Before they jump in and begin misbehaving, most students wait and see what you are like as a teacher. Their judgment is very quick and often very accurate. Students are experts at telling which teachers are pushovers and which are not. Therefore, it is important to make a good first impression. Remember, it is much easier to relax rules at some later date than to create new rules as the year goes on.

The key is to start strict, much stricter than you normally would. This does not mean that you cannot have a sense of humor. In fact, a sense of humor is one of the most important ingredients to good classroom management. However, it does mean that you have rules and that you enforce them fairly and consistently.

Students Test the Water

You have made a good impression, and students feel that you will be strict but fair. Yet many students will still test you. Like children going through their terrible twos, they want to see just how far they can push things before they are pushed back.

QUESTION

Should I tell students that I am new to teaching?
The best way to handle this issue is to play up your previous experience, even if it was just interning. Emphasize that you are new to the school, and avoid saying that this is your first full-time position.

Misbehavior at this early stage of the school year starts small. The way you deal with these small disturbances will determine the extent of larger misbehaviors later in the year. If you ignore the behavior, it will grow until you are forced to deal with it. By acting now, you will save yourself a lot of time and headaches later.

If you have a student on the first day who is really misbehaving, it is perfectly acceptable to send him to the office. This will definitely make an impression on your other students. It is better to let students see that you know what they are doing and that you have higher expectations for them. You will get huge results and rewards in the long run.

Habits of Successful Teachers

What makes a teacher successful? Many people feel that a successful teacher is someone who is well organized, creative, and has detailed lesson plans. While many effective teachers do share these habits, they are not enough. In fact, some successful teachers are unorganized. Some just seem to always be flying by the seat of their pants. However, their lives would be much easier if they did learn to be better organized and to plan more detailed lessons.

So if organization, creativity, and detailed lesson plans are not enough, what qualities do successful teachers possess? The ingredients for success include the following:

- Sense of fairness
- Consistent approach
- Ability to be flexible

- Positive attitude
- High expectations for yourself and your students
- Sense of humor

The first three of these are skills you practice each day. The second three should become part of your overall personality. All of these characteristics can be achieved through experience and practice. The strategies in this book will help make these attributes a part of your effective teaching repertoire.

Don't Be Afraid to Succeed!

Teaching can seem a scary endeavor. However, even if you do not feel confident when you walk into your classroom, you need to follow the old adage and "fake it until you make it." In other words, pretend that you are confident, and eventually you will gain confidence. Once you have mastered the technical aspects of teaching, such as paperwork, discipline, and lesson plans, you can really begin to reap the benefits of teaching. You will find that it is a very worthwhile and rewarding endeavor.

CHAPTER 2

The Secret Formula for Success

The way teachers define success varies widely, but you may think of success as being an effective teacher with a fulfilling career. The "secret formula" for success presented in this book involves six major ingredients: expectations, humor, attitude, consistency, fairness, and flexibility. Expectations will be covered in Chapter 3. Humor is discussed throughout the entire book. This chapter focuses on attitude, consistency, fairness, and flexibility.

With an Attitude

Every day, you set the tone in the classroom by your attitude. You are on stage from the moment your students arrive until the bell rings and it's time for them to leave. If you have a negative attitude, your students will also adopt this mindset, and your class that day will probably not be very productive. On the other hand, if you have a positive attitude toward your students, your subject, your profession, and yourself, you will find that this optimism pervades the class. You will probably have a productive day.

Attitude Has Positive Effects

The effects of a positive attitude have been widely studied. They include the following:

- Improved job satisfaction
- Better self-esteem
- Improved personal interactions
- Better health
- Greater achievement levels
- Improved overall happiness

People with positive attitudes are often healthier and happier in their jobs and personal lives. They typically can achieve more in any given day. People want to be around other positive individuals.

Everyone has probably experienced what it's like to be around a negative person. Just think how your students are going to feel after spending time with you if you are pessimistic about them or your curriculum.

The Core Aspect of Successful Teaching

While your attitude is just one part of the formula, it holds the core position. When you have a positive attitude, consistency, fairness, and flexibility are much easier to master. You will find that students will become more positive in their attitude toward you. A quick way to appear positive even if you do not feel it is to smile. You will find that if you smile, your attitude will follow, and you will be a happier person. Children need to feel loved and accepted. Your smile, kind words, and accepting attitude will go a long way toward helping your students feel that they can achieve.

Practice Consistency

Consistency in teaching means that your students know what to expect from you day to day. Your rules do not change from situation to situation. You are not strict one day and easygoing the next. There are no surprises for your kids, and they do not have to feel like they are walking on eggshells. Consistency is important if you want to earn the respect of your students.

In a consistent teacher's classroom, students know exactly what is expected of them at all times, and there is no question of what will happen if they fail to live up to those expectations. Because everyone knows the consequences, and there is no doubt about the reaction of the teacher, misbehavior is greatly reduced. Students in a consistent classroom can feel safe and can focus on what is important—not on what mood the teacher happens to be in on a particular day.

Another benefit of consistency is an easier working environment for the teacher. As a basic example, if you always require your students to put their name, the date, and the homework title on the top of their papers, this will cause a lot less headache for you in the long run. You will find that recording grades is much easier when you have this information on each paper. However, this must be enforced from the beginning or students will not follow through. Thus, consistently enforcing your requirements and rules from day one will result in an easier time for you and a more organized classroom.

Avoid Idle Threats and Promises

Another important aspect of consistency is following through. If you tell your students that you are going to do something, then you had better do it or they will lose respect for you. It is very important that you do not threaten your students with actions that you will not or cannot take.

Let's say your class is misbehaving during a quiz, and that some students are being particularly disruptive. If they don't buckle down, you say, everyone will get a zero. This is a good example of an idle threat. Realistically, it is not something you should or even would do. For one thing, your administration might have a real problem with this action, especially after parents begin calling. Plus, this punishment is unfair to the students who are not being disruptive.

ALERT

If you teach your students one thing and then do the opposite, you will not achieve the results you expect. To reinforce your expectations, it is important that your actions and words be consistent.

A Day-to-Day Practice

You will have bad days as a teacher. You will come to work unhappy about something that happened at home. Or you may not be feeling well. But even if you're having a bad day, you should try to be consistent in your actions and reactions. In fact, these days are the measure of your consistency.

Obviously, you will have moments when you react in a manner that is not truly consistent. You might lash out at a talkative student on a day you have a bad headache. But the less frequent these instances are, the more your students will respect you and the more effective you will be.

A Fair Deal

It is hard to determine whether consistency or fairness is the more important skill for a teacher. Students do not respect inconsistent teachers. However, they have a real problem with teachers they perceive as unfair. If you think back to your time as a student, you can probably remember at least one teacher you or your fellow students thought was unfair. This might have been someone who favored a certain group of students or someone whose rules seemed almost arbitrary. In the end, though, this teacher probably lost the respect of most students.

What Fairness Means in Practice

Fairness pervades your classroom environment. Students are very perceptive and will judge how fair you are as a teacher based on your daily actions. If you consistently enforce rules in the same manner for all students, then you will be perceived as fair. However, if you allow one student but not others to make up late work, this will be seen as unfair by your class.

Are there situations in which you want to act in a manner that might be seen as unfair? Sure there are. It can be very tough, for example, to enforce a rule broken by a normally excellent student. So, you need a hierarchy of response built into your system of positive and negative reinforcements. In other words, as a student breaks more rules, the punishment should change. This will help you in your effort to be fair. The student who makes one mistake will not be punished the same as one who makes many.

ESSENTIAL

Whether accurate or not, students have their own sense of what is fair. Realize that your goals are not necessarily the same, but remember that a perception of fairness is very important. Therefore, take some time to observe and talk to your students to determine their attitudes about fairness.

It can also be very difficult to act fairly to a student who is normally disruptive. However, experience proves that if you treat each day as a clean slate in terms of your reactions to the students, you will find that their behavior will not be quite as extreme. If there are students who are perpetually in trouble, they will expect you to treat them more harshly, thus giving them no incentive to try to act better. However, if you surprise them by not holding grudges, you in turn may be pleasantly surprised by the results. This does not mean that students should go unpunished for their offenses. It just means that you need to watch your actions and attitude when approaching these students each day.

Fairness Is a Learned Behavior

It is possible to train yourself to be fairer as a teacher. Take stock of your actions at the end of each day to see where you might not have acted fairly. Give yourself time before making decisions concerning discipline in your classroom. Sometimes giving the disruptive student and yourself a cooling-off period will allow you to approach the situation more rationally.

Everyone makes mistakes, and no one is fair all the time. However, students will notice and appreciate your attempts to treat all students equally and with an equal measure of respect every day.

Learn to Be Flexible

A teacher who is inflexible will not survive very long in the profession without burning out. No day is typical in the life a teacher. Very few lessons go exactly as planned. Interruptions can ruin the momentum of a class. Student disruptions can upset you and others, placing learning on the back burner.

If you have not prepared yourself to be in a constant state of flux, then you need to re-evaluate your choice of profession. Instead of looking at this instability in a negative light, it is important to see the positives in the situation. Change is necessary and exciting. Each day presents new challenges to overcome. Necessity is the mother of invention, and you will find that you invent many new techniques and ideas to help you adapt to the changing atmosphere of the school.

Keep Your Sanity

Teachers are suffering burnout all over the nation. In fact, it is estimated that 50 percent of teachers leave the profession in their first five years of teaching. This number is so high because teaching is a stressful job.

Unfortunately, you cannot change the school system, the interruptions, or the disruptions that will occur in your class each day. What you can alter is your own attitude about these disruptions. Being flexible and adaptable will help you deal with the many stresses of the job while allowing you to keep your sanity. If you look at many disgruntled teachers, you will see inflexible individuals who do not want to change their outlook or teaching methods.

The Flexible Lesson Plan

Take your lesson plan as an example. Many teachers make the mistake of treating the lesson plan as though it's set in stone, the only way of teaching their class. However, a lesson plan is not a strict regimen that must be followed. Really, it's nothing more than a guide.

Let's say you have created a multipart lesson plan for a high school course that only allows for a twenty-minute discussion period. However, once the discussion actually begins, the students get really involved. They are enjoying the conversation, and there's a lot of learning and interchange of good ideas going on. Do you decide at this point to cut the discussion short to follow your schedule or do you allow the discussion to continue so as not to lose momentum?

FACT

If you teach in a high school that offers fifty-minute classes for 180 days, you may think that you have 9,000 minutes of instructional time. However, after taking daily routines and expected or unexpected interruptions into account, you will probably be left with closer to 7,600 minutes (or 153 days) devoted to teaching.

Obviously, you want to allow the discussion to continue. Moments like this can be rare, and they are wonderful to behold when they happen. It is your job as a teacher to capitalize on your class's excitement and not be hemmed in by a lesson plan you wrote the week before.

Many secondary school teachers get concerned if they do not cover the same material with each class and one falls behind. This can be confusing. However, you can adapt your lessons for that one class to gain time somewhere else. It is a small price to pay for a great educational experience.

Putting It All Together

Combining a positive attitude, consistency, fairness, and flexibility with high expectations and a sense of humor can be quite a balancing act. It is important to realize that finding this balance is often the result of trial and error. However, if you work hard each day to achieve these goals, you will be well rewarded with a much happier classroom environment.

Your Own Teaching Style

No two teachers are alike, just as no two people are alike. Teachers come from different backgrounds, and they have educational memories and experiences that shape their attitudes about teaching. Realize that the teaching methods used by your own instructors may not work for you or even be sound educational practice.

ALERT

You should approach every day as a new opportunity to grow and achieve your goals. Above all, try to have fun. Teaching should not be drudgery but should be full of exciting opportunities for sharing and growth.

It is fine to work with mentors and to emulate some of their best qualities. However, you will be happiest and most successful if you take the information presented here and combine it with the advice of experienced, effective teachers to create your own teaching style. Look for positive teaching skills in each teacher you meet, and include them in your own practices.

Dealing with Mistakes

All teachers, even those who are most effective, make mistakes. There will be occasions when your attitude is bad no matter what you do, or when you are inconsistent, unfair, or inflexible despite yourself. These can become learning opportunities if you handle them the right way. It is not wrong or a sign of weakness to admit that you made a mistake or to apologize to your students, if necessary. Once the incident is over, move on with a renewed commitment to avoid that mistake again.

The best teachers are the best learners. Allow yourself the opportunity to learn as you teach. You learn from books, certainly, but your everyday life in the classroom also offers lessons on personal and professional growth. Mistakes allow you to grow. If you did everything right the first time, you would never have anything to learn. Mistakes are opportunities that can become your springboards to newer heights.

Practical Applications

Reading about these techniques and habits is one thing, but seeing how they work in practice is another. Walking through a few examples will allow you the opportunity to reflect on how you would react.

Following are several real-life scenarios that you might encounter in the classroom. The correct answers to the questions might seem obvious according to what has been discussed so far, but it is important to truly reflect on your instinctive reaction. In the heat of the moment, your instinct may not be the best reaction. Your goal should be to prepare yourself before these events occur.

Role-Playing Attitude and Flexibility

It's the first day of school. You have forty-one students in your class, but there are only desks for thirty-two. There is also a small table with four more chairs around it. That leaves five students without a place to sit. What do you do?

a. Complain out loud to the students that there is no room for them and they will just have to sit on the floor.
b. Send students out to other classrooms looking for spare desks and chairs.
c. Smile and make a joke about the lack of space while keeping an upbeat attitude that it will all be fixed in a few days.
d. Make no comment concerning the situation and get right down to the business of the first day.

The best answer is *c*. By smiling and trying to make the students laugh about the situation, you make kids who might feel uncomfortable or unwanted feel welcome. Your flexibility will allow you to adjust to this situation and to realize that it will not last forever.

If you answered *a*, don't worry. This is probably what most teachers would be thinking to themselves. However, complaining to the students—even if you are not telling them to leave or explicitly saying they are not welcome—will make them feel unwanted. This is especially true with younger students who might not understand and think your comments are directed at them.

Answer *b* would definitely not be the best solution because other teachers around you are probably in the same situation. It is never a good idea to send students on such a mission because it interrupts others' classes and instructional time. It also creates a situation where students are roaming the hallways unattended. Finally, if you chose answer *d*, then you are not making a horrendous mistake but you are also not winning a lot of students over to your side. Show that you have a sense of humor, and it will be well appreciated.

Role-Playing Consistency

You catch two students cheating on a test. Student A is normally a great student who has never been in trouble before. Student B is normally a trying student who has been in trouble a few times, though never for cheating. What do you do?

a. Give both students a zero (or follow whatever rule you have established in the class for this sort of act).
b. Give both students a zero and write a referral for Student B (that is, send her to the dean, principal, or another designated administrator).
c. Give Student B a zero, since she has a history of causing trouble in your classroom. At the same time, verbally warn Student A that you do not want this behavior repeated again.
d. Ignore the situation completely because you do not want to get Student A in trouble. Later, discuss the incident with Student A in private.

The best and most consistent answer to this question is *a*. Even though you might like Student A or think that the incident was an accident, you must consistently follow the rules you have established. If Student B has had previous offenses with cheating, then obviously *b* would be an okay answer. However, in this instance that was not the case.

Answer *c* is the most inconsistent of all. It would definitely be seen as favoritism by Student B and her friends. Further, the situation would be even harder on Student A, who might be seen as a favorite.

Finally, some teachers might opt for *d*. However, no conversation should ever be considered private between a teacher and a student. In most cases, the student will tell a friend who will tell a friend until eventually it gets back to the other student. This response to the situation has the potential to blow up in your face.

FACT

In a recent survey, 80 percent of high school students said they had cheated in school. While cheating occurs less in elementary school, as students advance and grades become more important, incidents of cheating increase. You must come up with a consistent method for handling cheating because you will be faced with it many times in your teaching career.

Role-Playing Fairness

A student who has always had an attitude problem in your class gets up one day in the middle of a lesson, cusses at you and calls you bad names, and then storms out of the room. He gets ten days of out-of-school suspension for the act. When he returns to class after his suspension is over, how do you react?

a. You treat him coldly, upset at the things he said to you.
b. You ignore his return and don't address the incident with him at all.
c. You make a joke about his return, hoping to smooth things over.
d. You meet with him privately to say that as long as he can promise to keep himself under control, you will pretend that nothing happened.

The best answer is *d*. You do not disrupt your class to deal with the situation, but you make sure to address it with the student, no matter how uncomfortable you may be. It might be difficult, but if you can let go of your hurt and anger and start fresh, he just might turn around.

Answer *a* would just make matters worse. You are the adult in the situation. It is important that you behave as one, or you have already lost. Power struggles should be avoided at all costs. Many teachers might be tempted to choose answer *b*. It is an awkward situation when students return after a referral, but it did happen, and ignoring it will leave the event unfinished. It is best to get it over with so you can go back to what is really important:

teaching students. The only time this might be a viable option is if physical violence was threatened.

Answer *c* could be taken one of two ways, depending on the personality of the student in question. However, because the situation is a volatile one, a joke could seem condescending and sarcastic. It is best to steer clear of this answer. Maybe someday when things calm down, you will be able to joke with the student about the situation.

CHAPTER 3

From Expectations to Results

The expectations that you set for yourself will determine your actions. If you expect to succeed, you will likely do so. Likewise, if you expect to fail, you definitely will. This is especially true in the classroom. If you expect and believe that your students will succeed, you will probably find that they live up to your expectations. And your attitude can be infectious; students will take their cue from you on what to expect of themselves.

Great Expectations

Many teachers believe they know how much their students can learn. Rather than being based on the actual skills of the students in question, these beliefs are often formed from other sources of information. They might come from discussions that they have held with other teachers about students in their class, the number of students they are teaching who are involved in "pull-out programs," the level of the class as listed on the course information sheet for high school teachers, or even personal biases about students in general.

If a teacher walks into a classroom with the attitude that the students cannot learn the material for the course, the battle is lost before it has begun. Low expectations serve as a self-fulfilling prophecy, resulting in lower student achievement and interest. On the other hand, if a teacher believes that the students can learn the material, then the students will pick up on this, and it too will become a self-fulfilling prophecy.

Your Attitude and Demeanor

Students are very smart at picking up the nuances of individual teachers and their opinions. If you truly believe that all the students in your class can learn the material required for the course, then your attitude and demeanor will reflect that belief.

Teachers with high expectations typically smile more, joke more, and encourage more. They have a "can-do" attitude and probably achieve more in their own lives, too. Students who have high expectations for themselves end up believing in their own ability to learn. No student wants to feel dumb, but when teachers do not offer the opportunity to achieve, some students do start to feel inferior.

High Expectations or Unrealistic Demands?

High expectations are necessary and they result in positive achievement, But impossible expectations set students up to fail. This is an important distinction.

Many difficult concepts rely on background knowledge and previous academic experience. If a student has not successfully completed a required prerequisite for the course you are teaching, she doesn't have the tools she needs to succeed. It would be impossible to expect her to master the concepts without much remediation. For example, if a child does not understand the basics of addition, they cannot be expected to comprehend multiplication. Similarly, if she has never studied algebra, then she will have a difficult time with some concepts in chemistry.

ALERT

The students who are the worst hurt by impossible expectations are those of low ability and low achievement. Many of these students already have self-esteem problems. However, these same students' self-esteem can benefit greatly from high, yet attainable, expectations.

Do not assume, however, that this student cannot learn. Instead, try to think of ways to help this child get the required knowledge. If you are an elementary school teacher, you should schedule a conference with a parent or guardian so that they understand the difficulties their child is facing. You might offer additional resources like learning aids and possibly even after-school tutoring. In secondary school, a student who skipped over or failed a course could be placed back in that course for the remainder of the year if the problem is recognized early. If a student needs tutoring, most schools offer teacher or student tutoring at various times. Just remember, your attitude about the student's situation will form her attitude about whether she has the ability to learn.

It is also imperative that you base your expectations on the group of students you are teaching. Elementary school teachers typically have testing results to help them determine the general ability of their students, which can guide the amount of time spent on foundational topics. High schools generally offer regular, honors, and even advanced placement courses in a subject to meet the needs of different students. Your expectation should be that all students enrolled in your course will learn the information you are going to present in a manner suitable to their ability.

Fears Associated with High Expectations

As educators, it is important to change the perception that high expectations set students up to fail. They don't—but low or impossible expectations do. Low expectations can create a false sense of accomplishment that is not based on reality. High expectations, however, can lead to authentic and heightened self-esteem.

ESSENTIAL

Critics argue that high expectations can lead to failure. But what effect do low or no expectations have on students? Students' motivation to learn is shaped by their attitudes toward learning, which in turn are largely shaped by their parents and by you.

Students need to feel that you believe they can learn. Having high expectations does not mean that a student is a failure if he does not understand a subject or has a hard time with it. It simply means that you expect him to try, and that with additional help, you believe he can succeed. Students who have never been respected academically will probably begin acknowledging your efforts through their words and actions.

Shedding Your Biases

Most biases are based on your past experiences and beliefs. Some are even based on your own fears about your abilities. In education, it is important to face your biases and determine whether they are valid or should be discarded. Here are some of the more predominant biased beliefs:

- Some students just cannot (or will not) learn.
- A good teacher must teach to the lowest/middle/highest student.
- Some information is too difficult for students to learn.
- Gifted students do not need extra help.

Any of these biases is enough to produce negative expectations and therefore negative results, both in your professional life and in the life of your students.

"Some Students Just Can't Learn"

This bias comes from the belief that learning is difficult. Look at your own perceptions: Do you believe that with enough time and effort you could learn anything? If you don't, your bias directly relates to your own fears. It is true that some topics are conceptual and might be beyond your students' current skill set. But you should still believe it is possible for them to learn that information, given time and effort.

ALERT

Be very careful to examine your biases. Even if you think they are hidden, your actions will reveal what you truly believe. Students will be able to pick up on your negative opinions, which could seriously harm the learning environment.

"Teaching to the Lowest/Highest Student"

You might have heard of the phrase "dumbed down." Many teachers water down their curriculum to be able to reach the lowest students, ignoring the needs of average- or high-achieving students. Other teachers choose to teach to the highest-achieving students in a class, thereby losing the lower students. The fact is that you should not specifically target your curriculum to one group or the other.

This is an extremely challenging task. Classrooms are often filled with students at many different levels. One way that you can reach more students is by varying your methods of instruction. You can also provide higher-achieving students opportunities to extend their knowledge. You may need to reevaluate your standards and expectations from time to time, but you should not lower them to the detriment of the middle- and high-achieving students.

"Some Information Is Too Difficult"

This bias deals with the belief that certain concepts should be left out or passed over because they are, in your opinion, just too difficult. Obviously, students progress over time through levels of cognitive development, and they are therefore not ready for all types of knowledge at once. However, this bias reflects your personal beliefs about the information and not whether your students are developmentally ready to learn it.

ESSENTIAL

Varying instruction is essential to effective teaching at all levels. Write lessons to appeal to different learning styles. This does not mean you must appeal to all learning styles every day. It simply means that by mixing things up a little bit, student attention will be less likely to waver.

Hoarding of knowledge is a common source of power among people. As a teacher, it is important that you do not become a gatekeeper to knowledge, allowing only certain students the privilege of learning. Therefore, when you make decisions concerning which concepts to stress and which ones to leave out, make sure that you are not making unfair judgments about your own or your students' abilities.

"Gifted Students Do Not Need Extra Help"

If you teach gifted students, you will run into a lot of teachers who believe that your teaching load is easier than theirs. This is based on the perception that since gifted students are smart, they are easier to teach and easier to deal with. Nothing could be further from the truth.

Gifted students share many characteristics and may be:

- Intrinsically motivated
- Inquisitive
- Able to conceptualize
- Quick at grasping new information

- Creative
- Organized
- Sensitive

These are all very positive qualities. However, many times these same qualities can lead to problems for gifted students. Students who are intrinsically motivated can also be strong-willed, believing they know more than others. Because of their inquisitiveness, ability to conceptualize, and ability to grasp information quickly, gifted students become easily bored and impatient with routine. Because of their creativity, they often seem different than the other students. Because of their desire to organize, they can be perceived as bossy. Finally, because of their sensitivity, they can sometimes overreact to a situation.

FACT

Typically, districts classify students with an IQ above 130 as gifted. This varies from place to place, and many school districts are moving away from IQ scores as the main determination for entrance into gifted programs. Instead, they take a more holistic approach that examines the child's characteristics and attitudes.

Obviously, teaching gifted students involves a lot more than just presenting higher-order thinking lessons. Many still need extra help to grasp some topics. Further, much of teaching gifted students deals with teaching emotional and behavioral skills. As a result, teaching high-achieving students takes a lot of effort on the part of the teacher.

Communicating Your Expectations

It is not enough to have high expectations for your students; you must also let them know what these expectations are. There are many subtle and not-so-subtle ways to help kids understand your expectations. Ultimately, communicating your expectations begins on the first day and should be reinforced on a daily basis.

Methods of Communication

Here are nine methods you might use to let your students know your expectations:

1. Get students to sign an "Achievement Contract" at the beginning of the year. The contract outlines what you expect of them and what they should expect from you.
2. As students work, give them enough time to find answers on their own, providing only hints and ideas instead of jumping right in to tell them the correct answer.
3. Periodically allow students to express in writing how they think they are doing in the course and what suggestions they have to make the class better.
4. Speak to students in a positive manner at all times, stressing that you know they have the ability to learn what you are teaching.
5. Try to get to know your students and allow them to see you as a real person; this attitude will motivate some of your students to work harder in order to please you.
6. Remain in charge of your students as their teacher, and do not allow yourself to fall into the trap of trying to be their friend.
7. Make your standards for assignments and activities absolutely clear by telling students exactly what you expect from them.
8. Make sure you let all students know that they can earn a top grade in your course if they work hard enough.
9. Promote mastery learning by allowing students to revise assignments that received low grades.

Probably the most important thing that you can do to communicate your expectations is to live up to the expectations of your students. Be consistent and fair at all times in your classroom, and you will model integrity to your students. They will better understand what is expected of them if they can see you living up to your own high expectations.

Reinforcing Expectations

Expectations must be reinforced daily. Sometimes students might need gentle reminders. At other times, however, you might need to stop the normal course of study to discuss your expectations for the students. Only through repetition and constant reminders will students' attitudes change. This reinforcement might seem redundant, but it is well worth the effort.

QUESTION

Should I communicate my expectations to my students' parents? Definitely. Students will have a much better chance to succeed if their teachers and parents work together. Parents need to know not only what you expect of their children but also what you expect of them.

Effect of Expectations on Behavior

Student misbehavior is one of the biggest fears of new and inexperienced teachers. New teachers are unsure of what to expect. However, if you go into the classroom expecting a high level of cooperation and behavior, you will have a better shot at achieving your goals. Approaching a classroom with fear and the belief that students will misbehave becomes a self-fulfilling prophecy. Those teachers who approach student behavior in a positive manner—without believing kids will always misbehave—are the teachers who have better classroom management skills and lower stress levels.

Effect of Expectations on Achievement

If you let students know that you believe they can achieve a high grade in your class, they already have one person in their corner. Similarly, if you let elementary school students and their parents know that you believe they can meet grade-level expectations in math and reading, you are setting up an expectation of success. Some students have trouble believing in their own abilities. By constantly reinforcing the idea that they can do it, you are helping them believe in themselves. Eventually, they will internalize the message. Of course, not all students will earn high marks in your classroom, but many of them will make a greater effort to do better than they have in previous classes. In fact, high expectations for behavior and grades work together to produce a much better learning environment. Students who regulate their own behavior based on your expectations are much more likely to work harder and produce better work.

Meeting Your Own Expectations

Setting high (not impossible!) expectations for yourself is important in setting yourself up to achieve your goals. It is a good idea to frequently reflect on areas where you need to improve your teaching. Set goals for yourself, and track your progress over time.

There are many benefits in defining your expectations. First, you will find that you are less stressed because you have a better understanding of what is important to you. Second, your attitude will definitely improve. You will be more positive about what you and others can achieve. Finally, your confidence level will rise. If you believe that you too can learn and achieve, then you will begin accomplishing your goals.

CHAPTER 4

Setting the Ground Rules

Before you begin your first day, you should have systems in place to deal with the housekeeping issues that arise. If you have to play catch-up and devise these once the school year has begun, they will not be nearly as effective. This chapter will help you to get organized and to prepare some tools that will make your life easier in the long run. You don't have to follow every one of these strategies, but you can use this information to help you determine which will work for you.

The Wisdom of Posting Class Rules

Creating and posting class rules is a good way to start students out on the right foot and create high expectations for student behavior. Through posted and reinforced rules, you will lower the rate of misbehaviors and increase teaching and learning time. However, this is true only if you actually follow through according to a posted discipline plan. (Discipline issues and plans are covered in Chapter 5.)

Keep Rules Short and Simple

Many new teachers make some common mistakes when they create their rules. First, they do not limit the number of rules. There is a reason that phone numbers have only seven digits—this is about the limit of how many numbers most people can remember. Aim for five good rules.

FACT

According to the latest study by the National Center for Education Studies, 22 percent of schools are overcrowded. Having too many students in a class leads to greater chances for disruption. In these instances, it is extremely important that you have clear, consistent rules that every student understands.

The second mistake that new teachers commonly make is creating rules that are too general. Experienced teachers who have a strong handle on classroom discipline might be able to effectively enforce a rule like "Respect yourself and others." However, it is much easier for a newer teacher to enforce the rule, "Keep your hands and feet to yourself." Following are some other examples of rules that you could choose from to use in your class:

- Keep your hands and feet to yourself.
- Be in your seat when the bell rings (at the beginning of class).
- Follow directions the first time they are given.
- Raise your hand and wait until you are recognized before speaking.
- Stay in your assigned seat unless otherwise stated.
- No cursing or vulgar or offensive language.

- Keep your desk and surrounding area clean.
- Respect other people's property. — *Listen to others.*
- Eyes front when the teacher is talking.
- Come to class with all books and necessary materials, including paper and pen.
- No personal grooming in class.
- Respect others by not talking when the teacher or other students are talking.

As you can see, there are more than five listed here. Some of these are aimed at younger students and some at older. Choose what is best for you and your classroom.

Whenever possible, it's a good idea to phrase your rules in a positive manner. This way, students know what they're expected to do, not what they are prohibited from doing. However, some rules like "no cursing" do not lend themselves to this type of phrasing without becoming too general.

Presenting Rules to Your Students

How should you present your rules to students? The first step is to have the rules posted in your room before the first day of school. They should be in dark, permanent marker on a poster board that is visible to all students. When students come in the first day and you are introducing yourself and your rules, refer to the chart on the wall. Every time that someone violates a rule, refer again to the chart as you explain what the student did wrong.

Reinforce Rules Daily

As a consistent, effective teacher, it is important to emphasize that your rules are the same every day for all students. If your rules are not specific and are difficult to enforce, this could be a problem. By always maintaining a consistent message about the rules, you are more likely to enforce them, and students are more likely to follow them.

Many teachers create their class rules with good intentions. However, some teachers fail to enforce the rules consistently. You'll recognize their classes by the chaos as soon as you walk into one. Remember, students will pick up on any weakness related to rule enforcement on your part.

What if you find that a rule is not working or that another rule is necessary? The rules might be written in permanent marker, but they are not set in stone. As the teacher, you can replace a rule if the need arises. If you have created the proper climate of consistency and fairness, the transition to a new and necessary rule should be relatively painless.

ESSENTIAL

It is important that students know and learn your class rules, but it is also essential that parents also be informed. A good habit is to send home a copy of your classroom rules for parents to sign. When parents are informed, fewer misunderstandings will occur.

Missing School Supplies

Not every student will come prepared to class with pencils, paper, and books every day. This will always be an issue in the classroom because students tend to forget "little" things like writing instruments and test dates. The question that you face as a teacher is the method in which you deal with the situation.

Two major schools of thought seem to exist on this issue. One is that students need to learn to be responsible. Therefore, if they do not come prepared, they should not be able to participate in the lesson or should receive some other form of punishment. The second school of thought is that a forgotten pencil should not keep a kid from learning. Your opinion on this topic will determine what course of action you are likely to take in your classroom. If you go against your natural instincts, you are more likely to fail at consistently enforcing the rule.

The Responsibility Argument

Students need to learn responsibility, and part of going to school involves deadlines, requirements, and mandatory participation. This experience helps students prepare for life after school. Teachers who follow the responsibility argument reinforce personal responsibility by having strict rules concerning forgotten items. These teachers will often not allow students to participate in the class until they have found or borrowed their forgotten material. Typically, the older a student is, the more stringently this rule is applied. Elementary school teachers might be wise to have students bring in extra pencils and paper at the beginning of the year to use if something has been forgotten.

The Participation Argument

Teachers with this philosophy believe that students should be responsible for their materials, but a forgotten pencil or paper should not prevent a student from participating. These teachers will keep a stock of pencils, papers, spare books, and other supplies to lend to students.

Stocking materials can get quite expensive because students will forget to return borrowed items. An effective measure to ensure kids do not walk out of the room with the item you lent them is to have the student leave something in exchange like a backpack, a shoe, or a lunch.

Some teachers have tried to make students pay for materials. However, you should use caution and check with your administration before doing this because taking money from kids can lead to huge problems for you. However, you might be able to collect enough extra items by asking for donations of materials from parents at the beginning of the school year.

Chronic Problems and Other Issues

When students are chronically without their required materials, you need to make sure that this is not a symptom of a larger problem. Try to determine if they have issues at home that are keeping them from bringing their items to class, or if it is just a matter of laziness or defiance. If you do find that there is a problem at home, then you should contact the guidance counselor.

Students leaving their books at home can often cause a real problem; not many teachers have extra books to lend. Therefore, you might need to come up with methods to encourage kids to bring their books to class. A great way to encourage compliance is to have random material checks. Every student who has the materials necessary for the course during a check gets extra credit or a piece of candy or another appropriate reward.

Dealing with Tardiness

Methods of dealing with tardiness vary from school to school, grade level to grade level, and teacher to teacher. The best systems are those that are school-wide and strictly enforced. For example, a high school might have a "tardy card," which allows students to be late to a total of three classes per semester. When the student is late, the instructor signs the tardy card. If the student does not have her tardy card or has reached the limit, then she gets a referral for tardiness. An additional component to this system really seems to motivate students: If they get through the semester without a single signature on their cards, the card gets entered in a drawing for prizes.

If your school does not have a unified policy or does not enforce the policy they do have, then it is up to you as the teacher to come up with a fair and consistent way of handling inevitable tardiness. There are various ways to handle this issue, and some methods are better and more appropriate than others. Some examples of methods used include locking students out of the room, giving detention for tardiness, giving on-time quizzes, and creating your own version of the tardy card for your class. Of course, special consideration needs to be given to those students who are chronically tardy due to circumstances beyond their control.

Locking Students Out

Locking late students out of your room may seem like a good method to get kids to be punctual, but it should be avoided for reasons of liability. If something should happen to your students while they are locked out of your room or if they should vandalize or disrupt other classes, you will be partially to blame.

Another problem is that the locked-out students will be missing out on your class work. Since many schools do not allow you to count tardiness as an unexcused absence, students would have to make up the work later. In the end, this would probably result in more work for all of you.

Detention for Tardiness

Detention can be held before or after school. For individual rather than school-wide detention, the students should come to your class at the appointed time for assigned work. This can be an effective method as long as you follow through and give referrals to students who do not show up for their detention. However, you need to be aware of a few issues.

First, if the student's detention makes him miss the bus, then you will probably need to call the parents to discuss this. Many times students have no way of getting to school early or leaving late. Second, detention means an additional commitment from you. You have to stay in the room with the student the whole time of his detention. Finally, some of the students who are tardy will probably be those with whom you have personality conflicts. The thought of spending fifteen to thirty minutes alone in a room with one of those students might not be that appealing.

Your Own Tardy Card System

Tardy cards can be effective, especially in secondary schools, if you have the system already in place when the school year begins and you strictly enforce it. The system is similar to the school-wide system already explained. You determine how many times you feel it is acceptable for students to be late to your class—two or three is a good number. Then you give each student a card, which you sign if the student is late.

An important component of the tardy card is the associated discipline plan. This lets students know what punishments they will receive if they forget or use up their cards. When that occurs, it is your job to follow through and enforce your plan. Therefore, make sure that your plan is something you are willing to do.

Giving On-Time Quizzes

One method that some teachers use in conjunction with other systems is to give periodic on-time quizzes. These unannounced quizzes take place as soon as the bell rings. They are very short and cover review material from the day before. Students who are tardy are not allowed to take the quizzes and therefore receive zeros. Check with your administration to make sure this is allowed. Alternatively, you could give extra credit for completing the quizzes.

When It's Not the Student's Fault

Elementary school teachers sometimes face a difficult situation when a student is frequently tardy or absent because of her parents. It can be very hard to blame a child for an issue that is really her parent's fault. If parents fail to send their children to school, the legal system can become involved. On the other hand, for daily tardies there is no real method to force compliance. Notes home and phone calls to parents sometimes help. However, depending on the situation, realize that you might be waging a losing battle. If you find this is the case, talk to your administration about the best way to handle the situation for your classroom and for the child involved.

ESSENTIAL

Whenever you institute a system for dealing with routine occurrences, make sure that it is manageable. If you cannot carry it out in less than a minute or two, you probably need to rework it so it takes up less of your time.

Late-Work Policies

You should expect your students to sometimes forget assignments and turn in their work late. Therefore, you should have a policy in place to deal with these late-work issues. As always, it is important to make sure that the administration will support the policy you create. Nothing is worse than giving a student a punishment according to your plan and then having the administration reverse your decision after a parent phone call.

Importance of a Late-Work Policy

Choosing to ignore and not penalize late work is a mistake. This will upset students who do turn in their work on time, and you will lose credibility. Why should the students who do not follow your directions get the same benefits as those who do? Conscientious students will conclude that there's no reason to turn their work in on time, or they might feel cheated by your lack of consistency.

Choosing not to accept late work at all will also lead to problems. What happens when a student has a legitimate excuse? To be consistent, you must not make exceptions to your policy. However, if your punishment does not seem to fit the crime, then you will not be seen as fair. Further, you need to examine your beliefs about the purpose of education. If you believe that the work is important enough to be completed, then you need to accept it even if it's late.

QUESTION

What if a student is chronically late turning in work?
If turning in late work has become an issue, then it is a good idea to call a conference with the parents or guardians, the student, and the guidance department or administration. Before you leave the meeting, work out the details of a solution for this problem.

Common Policies

Since a late-work policy is a necessity, your job is to come up with an effective and enforceable plan. You need to find something quick and consistent that does not require a great deal of bookkeeping on your part.

One plan that seems to work well is to allow students one extra day to turn in late work and to penalize that work by a certain percentage. (For example, you might take off ten or twenty points.) However, for this to be effective you need to have a system for turning in this work. You might tell your students that late work must be turned in before the bell rings. If you have a pen handy as you accept the late work, you can immediately mark down the penalty on the paper. That way you will not forget how much each assignment needs to be reduced.

Make-up Work Policy

Your policy for dealing with make-up work should be consistent with the school's policy on excused and unexcused absences. Most schools will issue a policy concerning make-up work, but if your school doesn't, then you need to come up with your own policy.

If students are making up work after an excused absence, it needs to be very clear to them what they need to do and when they need to turn in the work. An excellent way to accomplish this is to create an "Assignment Book." This is a notebook for each class in which you or a student you designate writes down what was covered during the day, including any homework. The absent student is then responsible for looking at the notebook the day he returns and writing down the assignments. If a handout is required, these should be available next to the notebook so the students have easy access to them. For younger children, you might want to have the handouts along with other important information and assignments stapled and ready for them when they return. Make sure to write a note indicating when you expect the work to be returned.

Restroom Use and Hall Passes

The last of the issues that you will commonly deal with in class are restroom use and other hall passes. Most schools prohibit students from wandering around campus, which is quite understandable. Therefore, school-wide hall passes are usually circulated. You should fill out a hall pass for each student leaving your classroom. That way, if an administrator or another teacher stops a student, they can see exactly where she came from and where she is heading.

Restroom Passes

It is up to you as a teacher to decide exactly how to handle requests to use the bathroom. Restroom use is a sticky issue. On one hand, you do not want to keep a student who really has to go. On the other hand, this privilege is easily abused. A good policy is to allow any student to use the restroom. If you feel that a student is abusing the restroom privileges, then you should discuss it with administration and the student's parents. Usually, this problem can be solved through quick intervention.

A big problem that results from allowing all students to use the restroom when they need it is that it can quickly become disruptive. There is nothing worse than holding a discussion and having a student raise his hand only to discover he wants to go to the bathroom. It is perfectly acceptable to require students to wait until you are at your desk or not addressing the entire class to ask to use the restroom. Of course, if you're aware that a student has a medical problem, then you should allow that student to have a special restroom pass for emergencies.

Finally, realize that with younger children the urge to go to the bathroom is often ignored until the last minute. If you are teaching kindergarten or first grade, it might be a good idea to have at least an extra pair of underwear and pants for a boy and a girl so that you are prepared if an accident should occur.

Hall Passes

Hall passes are different from restroom passes. Most schools do not want students randomly walking through the halls. You should strictly limit hall passes to emergencies or to circumstances in which students are required to visit the office or the guidance counselor. Liability is the main issue here.

ALERT

If a student leaves your class without a good reason and gets hurt or does something that is illegal, the administration will question you and your methods. You might even be subject to lawsuits if you are proved negligent.

In elementary schools, typically you will want to pair up students when you send them out of the classroom. Try to think about student personalities when you send them out together so that at least one of the students is more responsible. Further, make sure that they understand where they are going and how quickly you expect them to return.

In high school, you should allow only one student out of your classroom at any time. Some schools allow you to create a standard hall pass—possibly a wooden one or some other "permanent" pass with your name and your class on it. That ensures that only one student leaves the class at a time. However, this is not acceptable at all schools, so make sure it is at yours before you construct one for yourself.

CHAPTER 5

Behavior Management

Behavior management is one of the biggest worries of all new teachers. If you're worried about being able to control your classroom, it's important to remember that all you need for behavior management is the right frame of mind and an effective, simple-to-use discipline plan. Armed with the tools detailed in this chapter, you will soon find behavior management one of the least of your worries on a daily basis.

Beginning on the Right Foot

Effective behavior management begins before the first day of school, when you start preparing for students and devise your discipline plan. Many students will test you from the beginning, so every action you make during the first few days of school will set the tone for the rest of the year. This is not meant to put an inordinate amount of pressure on you, but it is a fact that you need to face. Therefore, you should be as organized as possible before the first student walks through your door.

Attitude and Demeanor

You must begin the year with an attitude of self-assurance. Always remember that you are the teacher and are in charge. Your attitude must be positive and full of high expectations. You should be friendly, but make it clear that you are ready to enforce your class rules.

If a teacher does not enforce the class rules strictly and consistently from day one, she will find it almost impossible to control her classroom. It is very difficult to become stricter, but this is the situation most new teachers get into during their first few years of teaching. New teachers usually follow this pattern:

1. They start off with the desire to have kids like them.
2. They lose control of their classroom environment.
3. They decide to tighten down on the rules.
4. They lose their sense of humor.
5. They lose their students' attention and respect.
6. Misbehavior increases.

A much better prospect is to start the year in a stern manner. That way, you can ease up as the year goes on. Students will appreciate a more relaxed atmosphere. They will also realize that if they do not follow the rules, a working system is already in place to curb their misbehavior.

You Are Not Your Students' Friend

In the secondary school setting, probably the biggest mistake that new teachers make is trying to befriend their students. If you have not taught before, you might be wondering why this is a mistake. The answer is that when your students lose the respectful distance of the student/teacher relationship, you lose control. This is especially true with older students. Remember, your job is not to get the kids to like you. It is to get the kids to respect you and to motivate them to learn.

FACT

Your school district will probably have a discipline plan based on the Student Code of Conduct. However, many times the day-to-day discipline issues you experience will not be included in that plan. Even so, make sure to review a copy of the discipline plan before the school year begins.

Keeping the above in mind, it is important that elementary school teachers especially understand the importance of creating a warm, loving environment. Many young children need that extra bit of comfort from their teachers to help them realize that they are in a safe environment. This does not mean that elementary school teachers should coddle or baby their students. It simply means that younger children will respond better to approachable, comforting teachers than ones who are too stern and cold.

Discipline Plans

An important part of behavior management is knowing what to do if a disruption occurs. Having class rules is not enough; you need to decide what to do when those class rules are broken. This is where the discipline plan comes in.

The best discipline plan is straightforward, easy to follow, and quick to implement. A good rule is the "three strikes" policy. This means that in most instances, the students will go through three steps to get to the highest tier of the discipline plan. Here's a sample discipline plan with three steps:

1. For the first rule infraction, the student's name is written on board.
2. After the second infraction, a checkmark goes next to the name.
3. After the third infraction, the student sits in time out.

This type of system needs to be adapted to the level of the students and your particular needs. Other examples of disciplinary tactics teachers often use include the following:

- Giving after-school detention
- Assigning sentences for the student to write
- Requiring the student to help clean the classroom
- Calling the parents
- Giving time out
- Sending the child to the principal, guidance counselor, or the administrator designated for disciplinary action

Once you have decided on your particular discipline plan, you need to post it where all students can see it.

Enforcing the Rules

You now have class rules and a posted discipline plan. However, that's not enough to maintain discipline—you need to follow through. When a student breaks a rule, you must follow the discipline plan you have in place. Only then will students learn that they are not allowed to break the rules.

ALERT

At some point, you may be forced to deal with a physical altercation between students. The best plan is not to act alone to stop a fight. If you are alone, send a student for help, and try to ensure the safety of yourself and those students not involved.

To be fair and consistent, you should follow the steps of the discipline plan for every student. With that said, there will be times when a student misbehaves so outrageously that you have no choice but to jump right to level three on the plan. For example, if you have a student who gets up in the middle of the class, cusses at you and the rest of the class, and then leaves, you would write that student a referral.

Avoid Interruptions for Discipline

As you teach your lesson, make sure that you don't interrupt the flow to enforce discipline. Your discipline plan should not require you to stop everything to deal with minor misbehaviors. For example, if two students are passing notes to each other as you are holding a class discussion, do not interrupt your class to discuss this with them. This can easily escalate the situation into a confrontation.

Instead, follow your discipline procedure. Keep talking as you write the students' names on the board. This might take some practice, but it is well worth it. It shows students that you have a handle on things even as you are teaching the lesson.

Humor Is the Most Effective Tool

It cannot be stressed enough that humor is your most effective tool as a teacher. Humor can defuse a quickly escalating situation. It reduces tension and allows your students to see you as a real person. You don't need to be a standup comedian, nor is your job to provide entertainment. But if you can find the humor in a situation, make small jokes here and there. You will find that students will listen closer because they find your class more enjoyable.

FACT

According to Jean Piaget's theory on the stages of cognitive development, most people do not reach the stage at which they can use and fully understand sarcasm until they're twelve to eighteen years of age. Using sarcasm with younger students and those who have nonverbal communication problems should be avoided.

As a teacher, you will discover that you cannot joke with all students equally. Some students respond really well to humor, and some do not. Younger children might not understand your attempts at humor at all. Therefore, it is important to size up your students and adjust your attitudes according to how they respond.

Don't Overuse It

Teachers often use sarcasm, which does have its place if appropriate. For one thing, students are so used to hearing sarcasm on television that it seems normal to them. However, if misused, sarcasm can easily hurt a student's feelings without your even being aware of it. Make sure that a student understands your humor before joking with him. If you do use sarcasm, try to direct it at situations and not people. The misuse of sarcasm can easily lead to the perception that you really do not care about your students.

Active Listening

An important part of classroom management involves your listening skills. Too many teachers do not actually listen to what their students are saying, and the kids quickly pick up on this. It is in your best interest to hone your listening skills because just the simple act of listening can help calm an escalating situation.

ESSENTIAL

In a confrontational situation, you can use humor to diffuse tension and allow the student to save face. If you don't, you run the risk of escalating the problem to such an extent that it may require more drastic actions.

Active listening is a learned skill that allows you to fully listen and respond to others in the most effective manner possible. It involves several steps. First, give the speaker your full attention. When that person has finished speaking, repeat in your own words what you heard. Then give the speaker a chance to correct your interpretation. This cuts down on misunderstandings, and it makes the speaker feel that you are really listening. Here is an example of active listening in action:

STUDENT: "What's the answer to number six?"
TEACHER: "You'd rather not figure out number six by yourself?"
STUDENT: "I don't know which one is the correct answer."

TEACHER: "You don't want to try and figure it out?"
STUDENT: "Is it 'red' or 'blue'?"
TEACHER: "You want me to tell you the answer?"
STUDENT: "Well, how can I find out which one is right?"

By first letting the student see that you understand, and then by adding a little humor, you make it clear that you are not going to give out the answer but you are willing to help the student work it out.

Positive and Negative Reinforcement

Much press has been given to the pros and cons of using positive and negative reinforcement, but most people do not understand what the terms really mean. Basically, positive reinforcement is praise and reward for correct behavior. Negative reinforcement is punishment coupled with positive experiences for correct behavior. Positive reinforcement is not connected to misbehavior, but negative reinforcement is.

Students respond more positively to praise than to punishment. You will find that a judicious combination of both forms of reinforcement will serve you best in managing your classes.

Positive Reinforcement in Practice

Studies have shown that specific praise is very effective, while general praise is not. In other words, saying, "Johnny, excellent job adding those numbers," is much better than saying, "Great job, class." Keep this in mind when you praise or reward your students.

To make praise mean something, it must be given at the appropriate time. For example, if a student has a partially correct answer, you should not heap praise on her for answering the question correctly. Instead, you should point out the part of her answer that is correct and then help her dissect the question to come up with the complete answer.

Another point about positive reinforcement is that it must be evenly administered. It's not a good idea to keep praising the same one or two students in the class. Remember, even if you don't mean to play favorites, it is what the students perceive that matters.

B. F. Skinner's theory on "operant conditioning" says that rewards are much more effective when they do not occur regularly. In other words, intermittent rewards mean more and have a greater effect than routine rewards. Students who never know when a reward might happen will behave better than those who know that you never give out rewards on Tuesdays.

Negative Reinforcement in Practice

The term "negative reinforcement" is often confused with punishment, which is not the same thing. Negative reinforcement occurs when a painful behavior is stopped or avoided by a new behavior. Thus, punishment is always coupled with positive direction.

Let's say you have a student who is frequently tardy. She is punished every time she is tardy, and tardiness becomes a painful behavior for her. If that student is early one day and she is met with a positive reaction from you, that's negative reinforcement. The more often she is early and experiences your positive reaction, the more likely she is to continue arriving early. It is not necessarily the punishment itself that caused the change but the punishment paired with positive reaction for correct behavior.

A Balancing Act

What should you remember about this discussion of positive and negative reinforcement? First should be the importance of your discipline plan. With that plan in place, you can make behaviors "painful" that you wish students to avoid and "pleasurable" that you wish to encourage. Then, when a student discovers that he can avoid an unpleasant experience by changing his behavior, he will be more likely to do so. This is a continual balancing act that is never quite perfect, but as a teacher, you should always be working toward achieving the discipline balance.

Appropriate Disciplinary Actions

The disciplinary actions you choose to take should be based on a number of factors including the type of infraction, the age of the students involved, and any extenuating circumstances such as whether the student has disabilities that might have been a factor in the problem. It can sometimes be difficult to determine the best course of action when students have caused disruptions in your class. Your posted discipline plan should be a guide to help you make these decisions. However, sometimes you have to take extra measures to ensure a safe and positive classroom environment for all students.

Behavior Contracts

What do you do when you are dealing with a seven year old who hits other children when she is angry? How about a student who constantly talks and disrupts your classroom? Every year you will probably have at least one challenging student in your class. Behavior contracts are a great way to provide those students with the extra structure and support they need to change their behavior.

Behavior contracts are typically made between the teacher, student, and parents. Parents' involvement is key in order to make these contracts truly effective. A good behavior contract will include your expectations for the child's behavior, consequences for misbehavior, and rewards for acceptable behavior. It also should be easy for you and clear for the student and his parents to understand how you're going to track the student's behavior.

ESSENTIAL

Try to make the behavior contract as measurable as possible. State exactly what behavior you are expecting from the student. For example, it is much more effective to state that you expect the student to stop talking while you are speaking to the class than to say that he needs to be quiet.

Behavior contracts should reward students for improved behavior and provide them with clear consequences for misbehavior. A good system of rewards is one of the keys to getting students to change their behavior. Make the system easy to follow. For example, they might get a prize from a treat jar or treasure box if they do not receive any negative marks on a given day. Consequences for too many negative marks should be equally clear. You might say that two or more negative marks would mean that the student would lose recess for a day. Keeping behavior contracts clear and easy to follow will help ensure their success.

Discipline Referrals

Referrals are an effective tool in middle and high school if they are used in a judicious manner. However, referrals should not be used for every infraction in your class. Using referrals for minor infractions will lessen the meaning and weight of referrals. A referral's role is to act as the strongest deterrent for students because they are no longer dealing with you but with the administration.

If you overuse referrals, the administration at your school may question your ability to handle discipline issues within your class and your classroom-management techniques. In addition, your students will receive lighter punishment if you overuse the referrals system. For example, if you turn in three referrals a week, the administrator giving students their punishments will probably be much more lenient than if you turn in only three or four referrals each year. When a teacher who rarely resorts to referrals writes one, the administration takes notice and realizes that this situation is important enough for their intervention.

ALERT

In some schools, referrals are only encouraged in specific cases. One reason for this is that the administration may see numerous referrals as reflecting poorly on the school. Do not let this keep you from writing referrals as part of your discipline plan when you feel it is in the student's best interest.

If a student has been given in-school or out-of-school suspension based on your referral, you should expect a bit of awkwardness when she returns to class. The best way to handle this situation is to run your class as usual, making sure to include the student in the discussion or lesson. Then, when you have a moment, talk to the student and explain that even though you do not approve of her past behavior, you are willing to act as if it never happened. In other words, you will not ignore future misbehavior, but you do not expect the student to misbehave either. If you meet the student with hostility, you will probably experience further misbehaviors. If the student meets you with anger despite your best efforts, then you might need to call in an administrator as a mediator. Also, a call to the parent can be very effective in these instances.

Parental Communications

Communication with the parents of students is one of the most neglected aspects of successful teaching, especially at the secondary level. The reason for this neglect is obvious and borne of necessity: Teachers often do not have the time to make the necessary phone calls to parents. However, if you want to ensure parental support and increase good behavior, find the time to make that phone call.

Get on the Phone

Elementary and high school teachers should make an effort to talk to their students' parents at least once each grading period. Phone calls are a quick and easy method of keeping the lines of communication open. Elementary school teachers should find the time to call and talk to each parent above and beyond the once or twice a year parent-teacher conference. You have fewer phone calls to make than a secondary school teacher but you will probably find that your phone calls will last longer, so you should set aside ample time for each call. However, even a quick hello can often help you find a new way to connect with students or learn something important about what's going on in their lives. The importance of communication was demonstrated by a phone call with a third grader's parent who revealed that the student had recently had three deaths in his family. This student had seemed more subdued of late and this helped the teacher understand the reason for his behavioral changes.

Because communication can be a lot of work in an already overloaded schedule, a secondary school teacher might consider dividing students into categories of need: high, medium, and low. High-need students are those who are having a very difficult time or who are having major behavioral problems in class. Medium-need students are those who are barely getting by. Low-need students are doing well.

You should definitely contact the parents of all your high-need students and set goals for yourself with the other two groups. For example, you might try to reach half the parents of your medium-need students and maybe a quarter of the parents in the low-need group. Parents will respond favorably to your calls, and you will see an improvement in the quality of behavior and work.

ESSENTIAL

Secondary school teachers have to reach many more parents. One method for making phone calls a little more manageable is to divide the total number of students you teach by the number of weeks in a grading period. If you have to call 150 students in a six-week grading period, then you would need to call twenty-five parents each week to reach them all.

Provide Written Communication

Elementary school teachers will find that daily written communication with parents can be a huge boost to classroom behavior. If your students take home a daily agenda, then you can simply write a brief note to parents when their child is misbehaving. For example, if you have a student who has a habit of talking while you are talking, write this in her planner and require the parents to sign that they have read your note.

It is important not to overuse this type of note to parents. Do not send home a note every time you have to write a student's name on the board, for example. Instead, use it when you feel that parental involvement could make a difference with student behavior.

Parent-Teacher Conferences

Nothing can replace sitting down one-on-one and talking to the parents of your students. A conference is a good opportunity to share with parents your methods for lessons and grading as well as discussing the quality of their child's work. However, parent-teacher conferences can be very stressful. Some teachers find it difficult to be questioned by parents. Further, if parents are not responsive to your observations, they can become confrontational.

To prevent a negative reaction, it is very important that you come to parent-teacher conferences prepared. If you are meeting over a behavioral issue, it is often helpful if you call and talk to the parent on the phone before the conference so you have a basis for mutual discussion once the conference starts. You should be honest about your concerns and observations, but you should also be tactful in your delivery. Some parents will probably react with denial because it is easier than acceptance.

Another effective technique is to arrive at a parent-teacher conference with a plan in mind to help a struggling student. It is important that you and the student's parents work toward the same goals, because if you are clashing, the student will definitely pick that up and capitalize on it.

CHAPTER 6

Prejudice, Controversy, and Violence

Sometimes teaching can be a very difficult profession because there are aspects that are beyond the limits of your control. While you can maintain a level of discipline in your classroom through consistency and fairness, you still cannot control the uncontrollable. Prejudice and controversy will probably arise, especially in upper-level classes. School violence is a serious issue that cannot be ignored. Dealing with these uncertainties is one of the challenges of an effective educator.

Prejudice in the Classroom

Students come into your class from diverse backgrounds and they all have prejudices. As you teach, you will witness these prejudices surfacing and sometimes even causing problems within your class or the school. It is your job to keep your classroom as prejudice-free as possible. Prohibit stereotypes and put-downs in your class, and set an example by making sure that you do not rely on stereotypes either.

Your Reaction Sets the Tone

The first clue that students have to your staunch attitude against prejudice should be your initial reaction to any stereotypical or prejudicial statements. For example, if a student says something derogatory about immigrants, your reaction should be firm, swift, and forceful.

This does not mean that you should yell or become uncontrollable. Instead, with a serious expression, stare at the student in question and say something such as, "That type of speech is not allowed in this classroom." You will have an impact.

ALERT

While your reaction should be swift and firm, it should be fair. Unless a student has a history of inappropriate speech, you should assume that an expression of prejudice is a mistake and she did not realize the implications of her words. Use this opportunity to teach your students why the statement was inappropriate.

You need to be quick to stop offensive speech. If it gets out of hand, there will be hurt feelings and your classroom could become a battleground. This, of course, is to be avoided at all cost. Your classroom should be a safe haven for all students, and they should feel welcomed regardless of their gender, religion, or ethnic background.

You'll need to realize that elementary-aged children might not understand the full meaning behind their prejudicial statements. They might be repeating something they have heard outside of the school environment. Therefore, an effective teacher should use these moments to help students understand that prejudicial statements could hurt someone's feelings and are not appropriate. If the behavior continues, then further action should be taken, such as a phone call home or a parent-teacher conference.

Freedom of Speech

The older your students, the more likely that they will argue with you concerning their right to voice their opinions. Students often bring up the Constitution and its protection of free speech. Point out that they do have the protection of the Constitution, but according to the law, school is a special place. The Supreme Court has said that speech that "materially and substantially" disrupts class is not allowed. Any inflammatory speech against a group should be considered disruptive to the learning environment.

The Most Effective Tool

There are many ways that you can create a prejudice-free atmosphere in your classroom. For one thing, you should be very welcoming to all students on the first day of class. You can also discuss the issue before it arises, announcing to your class that your room is a "prejudice-free zone." To make this idea more concrete and humorous for students, one of the most effective tools you can use is "The Box."

The Box is an imaginary space located outside the classroom door. Its purpose is to hold all the prejudices, stereotypes, and hatreds that students might have while they are in your class. Instruct students as they come into your room, to leave these ideas, opinions, and words outside in The Box. Ultimately, you hope that by using this tool, you can help students leave their prejudices behind even when they are outside your classroom.

Creating The Box

You create The Box on the first day of class by explaining its location and purpose to the students. Explain what you want the students to leave in The Box. Have students reflect on what parts of their belief system they need to put there. Maybe it is their racial prejudices. Maybe it is more of a prejudice against a certain clique in your school. It could even be prejudices against people of a particular religion or political group. Whatever their prejudices, students should understand they are not allowed to bring them into your classroom.

If you closely observe your classes, you will notice that most students really like this idea. Often they feel justified in their own prejudices because they feel that everyone else in the class is also prejudiced. If you remove this idea from the system, then you are left with much less prejudice.

The Box in Practice

The Box is a serious subject, but it works best if treated in a light-hearted manner. Tell a student who begins speaking in a stereotypical or prejudicial manner that he needs to "put it in The Box." Even though The Box is imaginary, students have been known to get so involved with this idea that they bring in their own "boxes" as props. Encourage this behavior because getting students involved will help produce buy-in necessary for The Box to work. Students who do not participate will need to be dealt with individually and may need further disciplinary action for inappropriate speech.

Discussing Controversial Topics

Controversial topics will probably arise in most upper-level and some lower-level classes. Some topics will be inappropriate, and you will want to stop those discussions as soon as they begin. However, there are times when you will want to address important, current topics. For example, if cloning is in the news, it might be a good time to discuss it in a government or science class. Your job as the teacher is to facilitate and lead the discussion in an appropriate manner.

Avoiding Stereotypical Speech

Be prepared to address the way students frame their thoughts when talking about controversial topics. For example, it would not be appropriate at any time during a whole-class discussion for students to begin teasing or name-calling others for their beliefs. Similarly, it would not be appropriate to allow students to speak in a stereotypical manner about others. It is best to require your students to prove any claims they make. In other words, if they are going to make an inflammatory statement, they should have the scientific proof to back it up.

It is also important that you, too, follow this precept in your class. Do not lump a group of people together to make claims about them. For example, do not say, "All teenagers need to learn how to drive better." Politics is another area where this could occur, and will be covered in greater detail later in this chapter.

ALERT

The meaning and context of words is continually evolving. Students today use many words to refer to each other that once were considered racial slurs. Still, if you feel a word is inappropriate and offensive, you should require students to avoid using it.

Holding Classroom Debates

Debates are an extremely important and effective tool for teaching students how to research and approach a topic. You should not shy away from them simply because they can lead to controversial discussions. You can minimize the problems associated with debates by following some simple steps:

1. Give students ample time to research their debate topics.
2. Make sure that students know that inappropriate comments and speech will not be allowed.
3. Give all students a rubric explaining exactly how the debate will be graded.
4. Explain on your rubric that points will be deducted for stereotypical speech and name-calling.
5. Make it clear that all points introduced in the debate must be backed up by credible sources and require students to turn in a bibliography at the end.
6. Strictly limit speaking time, and make sure that only one student speaks at a time.
7. Allow for guided, open discussion at the end of a debate to talk about any important issues that might have come up during the debate.

Debating can be a lot of fun and is very interesting for both the students and the teacher. But don't let the fun distract you—it is still up to you to keep the students focused on the topic and speaking in an appropriate manner.

Religious Matters

Religion is a very sticky subject because so many differing emotions and beliefs are involved. It would be good to remember that many of the world's wars began and were fought because of religion. Therefore, it is a good general rule for public school teachers to avoid the topic, if at all possible.

There are times, however, that you will be required by standards to teach world religions, especially if you are teaching social studies. The important thing to remember is to present world religions in an even manner, not making fun of or stereotyping any of them. Of course, the rules for dealing with religion depend on whether you teach in a public or a private school.

Public Schools

Because public schools are part of the government, public school teachers must faithfully follow the Constitution. This means that they may not "establish a . . . religion" through their classroom. In practice, this means that as a teacher, you must not impose your views and beliefs on your students. Federal courts have ruled that you may not even read a Bible silently during class, as this might sway a child's opinion about religion. Similarly, you cannot post or refer to the Ten Commandments in class.

What should you do if a student asks you a question about your religious beliefs? In general, your school district will probably advise you to refrain from discussing specific religious viewpoints in a classroom setting. But you can state your religious preference. For example, you could say, "I am a Baptist," as long as you refrain from explaining the tenets of your faith to students.

Suppose you wear a cross or a Star of David on a necklace and a student asks you what the necklace represents. You should answer simply that it is a symbol of your religion. It would be inappropriate to give the student an explanation of why that symbol is part of your religion.

Student-led clubs that require teacher sponsors are another issue deserving mention. The courts have ruled that if a school has any club or extracurricular activity, then it can have a religious club. Since most schools require each club to have an adult sponsor, teachers will often be asked to sponsor such clubs. This is allowable as long as the club is student-led and the teacher is there to monitor the meetings and is not more actively involved.

QUESTION

Can I pray or participate in religious activities with students?
Yes, as long as the group does not meet during school time and you are not acting as a representative of the school. You need to be careful to meet these standards if you choose to become involved.

Private Schools

Private schools are subject to different rules. Many private schools are religious in orientation and follow the guidelines set by their administration. They only have to follow governmental rules concerning their attitudes toward religion if they receive federal aid. For example, the federal government might help a private Catholic school by buying its math books. This is allowable as long as the math books do not espouse a religious faith.

Holiday Celebrations

Halloween, Thanksgiving, Christmas, Chanukah, and Easter. Each year, teachers across the country face how to deal with these holidays in their classroom. Students love learning about and celebrating holidays. When teachers integrate them into their lesson plans, this builds interest while continuing the learning process as the holidays approach. However, it's not so simple anymore to just have kids put on Christmas skits or paint Easter eggs in class. Many teachers have found that they have to be cautious when teaching about religious holidays.

Elementary School Celebrations

Elementary students are the most excited about holidays. Many of them still believe in Santa Claus and the Easter Bunny. Therefore, teachers will find that they almost cannot avoid integrating and celebrating the holidays in their classrooms. Methods for doing this range from simple changes like creating word problems and reading passages that focus on holiday themes, to holding classroom celebrations with treats and crafts.

Even though most students and parents want and expect holidays to be part of the classroom experience at this level, elementary school teachers still need to remember that they cannot espouse a specific religious doctrine in front of their students. Instead, they should be inclusive, creating a warm, accepting environment for all students. You might have students who are Christian, Jewish, Muslim, or hold some other religious worldview. Keep this in mind as you create your lesson plans. If you have concerns, talk with your administration or a veteran teacher at your school.

Middle Schools and Holidays

Middle school students, especially the younger ones, still enjoy celebrating the holidays in school. This is a great way to help keep their interest level high as they head to winter or spring break. Many teachers assign a wonderful lesson in which students research and creatively present information about the ways different cultures celebrate holidays. This is a great way to broaden students' perspectives while teaching them about other cultures and beliefs at the same time. It also helps you as the teacher appear more neutral toward any one religion.

Private School Issues

Private schools have different concerns when celebrating holidays in the classroom. Obviously, if a school is affiliated with a particular religion, then teachers will most probably be able to include those religious beliefs in their lesson plans. However, this will vary by school and you should check with your administration to make sure of their policies. This is especially true with Halloween. Some Christian denominations have begun asking their members to avoid Halloween or change the focus from witches and goblins to more of a fall theme. Thus, it is always best to speak with a veteran teacher or your administrator to find out what is expected of you.

Political Issues

Another topic that deserves special consideration is politics. While not as controversial as religion, politics can still cause teachers problems if not handled correctly. It is perfectly acceptable to share with your students your political party affiliation. However, it is not acceptable to stereotype or make fun of people whose beliefs are different than yours. Remember, many of these students' parents and families will have opinions that are diametrically opposed to your own.

It is best to avoid politics completely, if possible. However, this is not always feasible. Sometimes current events thrust politics into the spotlight, and if you're teaching a class like American Government, you must address political issues. In that case, be very careful that you approach these issues in a neutral manner.

ALERT

Students have the legal right to abstain from saying the Pledge of Allegiance. If your class says the pledge daily, it is best to make no comment on who does or does not participate. However, this does not mean that nonparticipating students can disrupt the class by talking during the pledge.

When dealing with students and their beliefs, use the Socratic method. Ask your students questions to get them to more precisely define exactly what they believe and why. This does not mean that you cannot guide discussions, but it does mean that you should try to avoid imposing your views on your students.

Dealing with School Violence

A book from CBS News, *The Class of 2000: A Definitive Study,* found that while 96 percent of students felt safe in their schools, 22 percent of those same students knew students who carried weapons to school. Crime and violence do exist, and they are not exactly rare occurrences at many schools. It is important that you have the facts and some ideas about what you can do to prevent violence from occurring.

Prevalence of School Violence

According to a survey commissioned by the U.S. Department of Education's National Center for Education Statistics (NCES), the overall rate of violent acts reported for elementary, middle, and high schools combined was 31 incidents per 1,000 students during the 2005–2006 school year. Further, 9 percent of schools reported student threats of violent attacks with a weapon. These seem to be scary numbers, but it is important to keep this in perspective. Only 3 percent of all students were involved in violent acts. Further, when you look at the serious violent acts of rape, sexual battery other than rape, fighting with a weapon, and robbery with or without a weapon, the number of students involved drops to 1.2 for every 1,000 students. There's no reason to become overly worried about school violence and crime, but make sure to take some time and understand what you can do to help prevent it.

What You Can Do

One of the main things you can do to help prevent violent crimes at school is to watch for warning signs from your students, which include the following:

- A sudden change in interest level at school
- An obsession with violence
- Sudden change in attitude or mood swings
- Clues from writing, including signs of isolation and despair
- Sudden violent and angry outbursts
- Talking about dying or death
- Talking about bringing weapons to school
- Indications of violence toward animals

If you see these signs in your students, report them to the guidance counselor at your school, tell your administration, and call the parents. This is an important issue that requires a proactive attitude. Also remember that you are a good role model for your students. Do not allow your own anger to get out of control; teach students good anger-management techniques when the occasion arises.

You will probably witness fights at school. Mostly, these will be isolated events, rarely with weapons or other dangerous items involved. Your main job during these incidents is to protect yourself and your students while trying to alleviate the situation as quickly as possible. Each school district has its own rules concerning how you should handle a fight, so make sure that you consult with other teachers and administrators before such events occur.

While you will probably see some school fights, you are not likely to witness major incidents of school violence. However, this does not mean that you should be unprepared. Your school should have a plan for dealing with emergencies; make sure that you are intimately aware of your role in that plan.

Worries about school violence should not stop you from teaching or from enjoying your career. Strive to create a safe environment for your students without allowing fear to cripple your teaching efforts. Awareness on your part will go a long way toward warding off violence and helping you and your students focus on learning.

School Bullying

School bullying is difficult to define—it can range anywhere from teasing and taunting to threats and outright violence. Bullying can happen in any grade, but it most commonly occurs in the middle grades. In fact, in 2005-2006, middle schools reported almost double the number of bullying incidents than either elementary or high schools.

Bullying can have extremely damaging effects. In fact, links were made between the horrible violence at Columbine High School in 1999 and school bullying. Outcast students feel disconnected, which can lead to frustration, low self-esteem, anger, and the need to lash out.

Solving the Problem

Your first task in dealing with this issue should be to find out how your school defines bullying. If bullying is a real problem, it is key that the administration and teachers come up with a consistent policy for identifying and dealing with bullies. Your school should not only deal with bullying when it occurs but also work on preventing it from happening. Following are some things that schools have done to combat bullying:

- Teachers include information about bullying in the curriculum. Some schools create special units that are covered in specific classes at the beginning of each year.
- Schools have worked on increasing community awareness. Pamphlets and other information focus on parents getting involved to combat bullying.
- Guidance counselors and other individuals make themselves available for students to talk about bullying. This allows students to express their fears and concerns.
- Schools that have bullying problems increase supervision in areas such as the lunchroom, the playground, and the parking lot. The increased adult presence can help decrease problems.
- Administrators have worked with the entire staff, dealing with sensitivity to victims and their families. Often, bullied victims do not see a way out of their predicament and actions that school officials take can sometimes hurt more than help.

ESSENTIAL

As a teacher, you will need to come up with an action plan for dealing with bullying. Realize that even though you cannot prevent all incidences of bullying from occurring, you are responsible for what goes on in your classroom. Ignoring this type of behavior is unacceptable.

On a more personal note, if you notice that certain students are often a target, pull them aside and give them some techniques that might help them deal with the situation. Often, simply agreeing with bullies or laughing at what they are saying will defuse the situation. Once an individual is

Chapter 6: Prejudice, Controversy, and Violence

no longer seen as an easy target, he will more than likely be left alone as the bully moves on to others who they feel can be overpowered.

In the end, bullying is a problem all educators must combat. If students do not feel safe in their school, how can they truly achieve their highest potential? Some teachers disregard teasing and taunting as a common, even necessary, part of childhood. However, to the child who is being teased, this "big picture" attitude means nothing. In fact, many of these students will be scarred for life because of what some might see as insignificant teasing. Bullied children need instant relief, and your care and concern can truly help.

CHAPTER 7

Organizing Your Space

An unorganized teacher often has a hard time controlling student behavior. On the other hand, a teacher who has devoted some thought, time, and effort to room organization will find many housekeeping issues easier to handle. Good organization will help you cut down on disruptions while maximizing learning time. Organizing yourself and your room does not have to be a boring task, so start the year with a good and convenient organizational system in place.

Setting Up Classroom Space

One of the most fundamental decisions you will make is how to organize your room. This includes the location of your desk, student desks, tables, bookcases, file cabinets, and any other items you have at your disposal. Before you make any decisions about specific items, it is a good idea to think of the utility of your room. For example, keep a bookcase with books you often refer to within arm's reach of your desk. Keeping that in mind, you can begin placing your biggest items first.

Seat Placement

Most likely, your room will have a blackboard (or whiteboard) along with an overhead screen. Therefore, this will probably determine the general direction your students will face. Traditionally, student desks are placed in rows. However, if you wish, you can try other methods of organization.

Some teachers like to place their students in blocks or even in a large circle. However, be careful of jumping into this sort of desk arrangement unless you have a strong handle on classroom discipline. Sometimes these arrangements can lead to more talking and less attention from your students.

ALERT

You should always keep some antibacterial cleaner on hand to clean off your desks. Custodians often do not have the time to clean student desks. It is a good idea to wipe the desks once a week in order to kill germs and keep things clean.

A good alternative is to arrange your students' desks in rows, but have them move their desks for special assignments and discussions. If you plan on having your students periodically move their desks for tasks (for example, if you ask them to move into a circle for classroom discussion each week), then it is a good idea to have your students practice quietly and quickly moving their desks into position. One word of warning: If you are going to have a lot of shifting desks in your room, be thoughtful of your neighbors. Have the students pick up their desks instead of just pushing them along the floor. You don't want to start shifting desks if the class next door is in the middle of a test.

Assigned Seats

It is in your best interest to assign your students their seats. This aids in learning names and also in keeping students under control. Teachers may go about this in a couple of different ways. Some teachers allow the students to choose their own seats, and other teachers choose the seats for the students.

If you allow students to choose their own seats, have them pick their seats on the first day of class. Create a classroom seating plan based on their choices, which becomes the seating chart. The positive benefit of this plan is that students like the freedom to choose their seats in the beginning.

ESSENTIAL

Pay particular attention when you're placing students with learning disabilities. For example, students with hearing and sight problems will need to be placed in the front row. Students who are easily distracted need to be placed away from possible distractions like windows.

The drawbacks to this option, however, outweigh the benefits. While it might be easier for you on the first day, it will probably cause you problems later in the year. Students will sit next to their friends, which will cause behavior problems. Poor-performing students who need extra help will usually choose to sit in the back of the room.

Assigning seats for your students is the other option. You prepare a seating chart before the students arrive, and then they sit in the seats you indicate. This option will probably cause some grumbling, but if you act matter-of-fact about it, your students will quickly adjust.

If you choose to pick where the students sit, you will probably want to adjust the plan as the year goes on. You should make this clear to the students. Explain that you will be making adjustments after the first two weeks and then once each grading period. That way, once you become familiar with your students, you can move them into the seats that will afford them the greatest opportunities to learn.

Placing Your Desk

Where you place your desk will greatly depend on the location of the chalkboard and student desks. There are numerous ways you can place your desk. Most teachers put their desks in the front of the room with the students facing the desk. It might be to one side of the chalkboard. This allows you quick access to the board and will allow you to look at your students as they work at their desks.

However, you are not required to place your desk at the front. In fact, many teachers find that placing their desks behind the students can be very effective. For one thing, if you allow students to choose their seats, usually those who need the most help or are the most disruptive will sit in the back, even if your desk happens to be located there. This can lead to better classroom control.

ESSENTIAL

Make sure that you have at least one lockable drawer or cabinet where you can store your personal effects and confidential information. Many people will be in your room when you are not there. Do not assume that anything in your desk—or classroom, for that matter—is private.

Another benefit of sitting behind the students is that you do not cause as great a disruption for them as they work. They will not be distracted if you shuffle papers or work on your computer. You will also have some privacy to complete other daily tasks.

Organizing Other Items

Now that you have placed the student and teacher desks, you can place the rest of your large items. As previously noted, think about each item's placement in terms of how you plan to use it. For example, if you need students to access certain books during class, try not to place the bookshelf behind your desk. If you have a file cabinet you plan to use frequently, try to position it close to your desk. That way, it will take less time and effort on your part to stay organized.

Decorating Your Room

Once the big items are in position, you can decorate your room. Most teachers have to pay for their own decorations, however, some schools do give teachers a small discretionary budget. At the very least, you will want to have some construction paper and a cardboard border to go around your bulletin boards along with a few posters or visuals that are connected to your curriculum.

Think carefully about possible distractions as you place posters and create billboards. There is a fine line between an interesting and well-decorated room and one that is so cluttered that students will have problems concentrating. If you find your students spend more time looking at your posters than working, you might want to consider removing some.

Classroom Supplies

You will probably inherit your teacher desk, a file cabinet, and some other large items that you'll find in your classroom. However, you will probably need to spend some time gathering additional necessary supplies. Usually, you will find experienced teachers on staff with extra supplies they've collected over the years that they are willing to share.

As you gather together your classroom supplies, you will definitely need the following:

- Chalk and/or markers
- Erasers
- Pens, pencils, and paper
- Pencil sharpener
- Stapler and scissors
- Thumbtacks and paperclips
- Tape and glue
- File folders

If you can get these items through administration or other teachers, then you have a good basis for what you need. Of course, you should adapt this list to your situation. Many teachers have access to an overhead projector, which means they need overhead sheets, markers, and cleaner.

Organizing Supplies

You will find that you will be better organized if you divide your room into separate areas. For example, you might have a location where all of your art supplies go. You could have containers containing rulers, glue sticks, markers and colored pencils, and construction paper. This will enable students to return materials to their proper place when they are finished.

Think about the different tasks you plan for your class before deciding on a final location for your supplies. Make a list of the top four to six tasks you and your students will complete that require supplies. Then assign each task a location in your room. The supplies associated with each of the tasks should be located in these separate areas.

Unique Supplies

Some subjects require teachers to store expensive supplies, such as graphing calculators and science materials. It is imperative that you have a cabinet with a lock or another secure container for these supplies. Unfortunately, expensive supplies often have a way of sprouting legs and walking away.

ALERT

As you place large items around your room, make sure that you do not block fire extinguishers or other safety devices. These must be accessible at all times. If you are teaching science, do not block the emergency shower so students can have quick access if any problem occurs.

It is also very important to have locked storage for potentially dangerous chemicals. It is a huge liability to leave dangerous substances in locations where students could easily get to them. Most schools have locking cabinets and separate storage rooms for science classrooms. If your school does not have these facilities, then you need to make a point of explaining the liabilities to your administration.

Textbook Use

Books are an important part of education, although some educational reformers have raised questions about the necessity of textbooks in classrooms. In fact, there is a movement in some places to eliminate texts altogether. It's true that many books are expensive and sometimes contain inaccurate information. Nevertheless, textbooks are important tools for all teachers to use as reference and teaching material.

New teachers are faced with creating a curriculum for their students. A good textbook is an important aid in helping them overcome the challenges of creating effective lesson plans each day. In fact, with all of the other obstacles and situations new teachers have to face in the classroom, a textbook can be a real lifesaver.

All teachers must use their texts responsibly—as a springboard to teaching important concepts and information. One of the reasons critics disparage textbook use is that many teachers rely on them as the only instrument of education. If that is the case in your classroom, and a textbook is the only instrument of education, you are not fulfilling your true role as a teacher.

Assigning Textbooks

It is important that you keep accurate records when you first assign textbooks to each student. Assigning textbooks in an irresponsible manner can lead to expenses equal to the cost of hiring a new teacher. To a lesser degree, it can cause a "book crunch" the following year if a school does not order enough replacement texts. New and experienced teachers must have a clear, easy-to-use method for assigning texts; otherwise it will eventually have very personal repercussions on the teacher.

Most schools will provide you with a method to organize book assignments. This will usually take the form of textbook cards. Use them to start off your organization method—you'll need to fill out the cards, organize them where they are safe, and deal with new student arrivals as the year progresses.

It is also a good idea to periodically hold textbook checks to ensure that students have not lost their books. By doing this early in the year, students will have time to find books they have misplaced. It also encourages students to keep track of their books.

Class Sets

Some schools do not have enough texts to provide each student with a copy to take home. This often happens at the end of a textbook ordering cycle. The school began with enough texts for every student, but through student growth, book damage, and attrition, the textbook count has dwindled. When this happens, teachers are forced to use texts from class sets.

Managing class sets can be a nightmare if you do not have a good system in place. This is because books have a tendency to walk out of the classroom with students. Rather than return the books they're using, many students simply forget and put them into their backpacks through habit. Therefore, you should create a system to handle assigning class sets to students.

One method you can use is to assign a book to each desk (as opposed to each student). It's easy to visually check at the end of each class to make sure all the books are there. Another method is to have the textbooks assigned to the students in the class. Each student has an in-class textbook card. You could house the books on a bookshelf convenient to the students, and they would be responsible for getting their book before the period starts. The students would then be responsible for replacing the books at the end of class.

Students Without Textbooks

On some days, at least some of your students will forget to bring their textbooks to class. If your lesson requires the students to refer to or read from their textbooks, you will have a problem on your hands. Your three options are:

- Not allowing participation without the required textbook.
- Allowing students to share their textbooks with others.
- Allowing them to check out a textbook for the day.

If you do not allow the student to participate, this could easily lead to distractions for the rest of the class. The student might become indignant and cause disruptions. And the education of the student would be lost for that period.

Sharing texts might work for certain assignments. For example, if you are reading a play out loud in an English class, the students could sit next to each other and read from the same book. However, this often leads to distractions between the students sharing the book, especially if they are close friends. Also, if your lesson does not lend itself well to sharing books—for example, students may be taking an open-book test—sharing might not even be a viable option.

ESSENTIAL

Many schools have multiple storage areas for textbooks. Sometimes there are numerous copies of the book you need just gathering dust somewhere on campus. Make sure to ask around for any "hidden" storage areas so you can check for extra copies of the textbook you are looking for.

If you are lucky, you will have the luxury of having a few extra textbooks to lend out to students who have forgotten their own. You should have a quick and easy system in place to handle this type of situation. For example, you could keep the textbooks behind your desk and have a sign-out sheet. Students who have forgotten their books sign out a loaner for the period. Then, if the book is not returned, you know who is responsible.

Checking Out Other Books

Many teachers have other books in their classrooms that they allow students to borrow and read. This is especially the case in language arts classes, where students are required to read other books for assignments. If you plan on having books that students can borrow, you need to create a checkout system.

Once again, make sure to create a system that is easy to understand and use. You should definitely restrict book checkouts to specific times in your class. Make sure that students clearly understand the procedures for checking out books in your class.

Keep a checkout sheet at your desk. You can choose to have the students be responsible for writing down the book's title, their name, the date, and the class they are in while you watch, or you can take care of writing it yourself. This provides you with a record of who has borrowed your books so you'll know whom to contact if they are not returned.

A Filing System

As a teacher, you'll find that you have to deal with a lot of paperwork. To stay organized, it's a good idea to set up a filing system. A good exercise is to write down all of the major file headings that you think you will need. Try to make them intuitive. You will not want to spend a great deal of time going through your files to find a specific paper because you cannot remember the file headings you used.

Try a color-coded system: pick a color for each of the major categories of files. For example, you might have different colors for the following:

- School paperwork
- Student work
- Lesson plans
- Curriculum-specific information
- Assessments
- Professional development

Once you pick the categories, you can create files using the color-coded category system and place them together in your file cabinets. If you see a file lying on your desk, you will know instantly what category of file it is.

FACT

If you would like to learn more about organizing your file system or your room itself, refer to *Organizing from the Inside Out*, by Julie Morgenstern. This book provides excellent systems to help you get your classroom organized.

Elementary school teachers often have to deal with several individual student assessments during the course of the year. As you create your filing system, you may want to give some thought to how you are going to report the information. You will probably want to have an overall file for each individual assessment type, i.e. reading tests, state assessments, etc., and then individual folders for each student within that assessment area. This system will help keep you organized and better enable you to use the assessment data in the future.

Making Your Life Easier

There are many other tools that teachers have been relying on to help create a more organized environment. As you begin teaching, make sure to ask your fellow teachers what systems work for them. Then adapt their ideas for your own use.

Student Cards

If you decide that you want to call a parent, where will you go to find the phone number? You could go to the main office. However, this information may be outdated. A better method is to create student cards on the first day of school. All you need are some 3" × 5" cards and a container. Give your students a card, and tell them all to fill out the information you wish to know. You can write the exact format on the board so that all the cards will be filled out in the same manner. Here's the kind of information you may wish to ask:

- Name
- Address
- Phone number
- Date of birth
- Class period
- Parent name
- Parent's work/cell number

Organize these cards alphabetically by period. You might even consider adding the student's assigned book number to the card so you have that information in one place.

A wonderful way to fully use these student cards is to mark down on the back any contacts you have with the student's parents. For example, you could record and date each phone call you made along with brief comments. That way, you will have a record for yourself or possibly even for administration, if a situation arises concerning the student.

Student Calendars

Having students fill out personal planners not only ensures that they're aware of their homework assignments, but it will also teach them an important life skill. It is very easy to create a blank calendar, print it out, and give one to each student. You should write an agenda on the board each day, and require the students to copy that agenda along with homework assignments into their calendar. Then, you can periodically collect and check the calendars for completion.

FACT

Some schools provide PTA or other volunteers to photocopy materials for teachers. Some do not even allow teachers to touch the copy machines. If this is the case in your school, you really have no choice but to plan ahead—it really is quite difficult to get those last-minute copies made.

A further benefit of this practice is that parents have a convenient record of what is occurring in your classroom. In your initial contact with a parent, you should explain the calendar system. You can continue to refer them to the calendar as the year progresses to help them remember upcoming events and see what work their students are doing. This reinforces the students' responsibility to stay organized and complete their work on time. Parents usually find this to be an effective and an extremely valuable tool for themselves and their children.

Copying Tips and Tricks

You will find that photocopying is often a time-consuming and frustrating endeavor. Therefore, if you plan ahead, you can take advantage of nonpeak copying times. Try not to wait until five minutes before school starts to copy today's exams. Arrive early or stay late if you are going to make necessary copies for a lesson.

Planning ahead with your photocopying needs is just another example of how good organizational skills and planning will mean the difference between a productive classroom environment and a frustrating one.

CHAPTER 8

Working with a Lesson Plan

The value of lesson plans cannot be overstated. They should not only serve as the framework of the daily lesson, but they should also be the road map for unifying your curriculum. Lesson plans come in many shapes and sizes, and some are more effective than others. Teachers who can turn a vision for their class into effective, flexible lesson plans will be more successful than those who cannot.

What Is a Lesson Plan?

A lesson plan is a framework and a road map, which each teacher will create using an individual style. A good lesson plan is one that sees the "big picture" but includes detailed information for each activity. It's a good idea to organize your lesson plan as a unit plan. Each unit plan will cover a particular topic, and may be broken down into daily plans. An effective unit plan will include the following:

- **Objective(s):** While easy to ignore, identifying objectives from the beginning will vastly simplify instruction and assessment.
- **Activities:** The meat of your lesson plan will be the various activities you use to teach students what you want them to learn.
- **Time estimates:** Including a time estimate for each activity allows you to divide your unit plan into days and periods of time.
- **Required materials:** Spend some time writing down exactly what materials you need for each activity so that you will be better prepared for your lesson.
- **Alternatives:** It is always wise to plan ahead for absent students, especially if a large part of your plan is a simulation that can be hard to make up for those who miss it.
- **Assessments:** Decide in the beginning how you are going to assess your students to help focus your instruction on what the students actually need to learn.

Unit plans are a good way of organizing your teaching. The beauty of putting together a unit plan is that you can go back and adjust activities as you get a better picture of the time needed for each day's lesson.

The Learning Objective

When a teacher takes the time to determine what he wants his students to learn from a lesson, he is creating a learning objective. These objectives help shape the curriculum and daily lessons of the course. Often, the learning objectives for a course are mandated by your district or state. The federal government publishes guidelines, which some schools ask their teachers to follow. Further, outside forces such as high-stakes testing can affect the learning objectives of classroom teachers. Overall, it is important for you as a teacher to combine these elements and add your own personal vision to create an effective learning environment.

State and National Standards

Each state has its own system for developing standards, and methods vary from district to district. While there are some national curriculum standards developed by different councils and groups, there are no "official" national standards that all teachers and schools must follow. Today, there are arguments both for and against the creation of national standards.

ESSENTIAL

Some school districts require standards to be listed on every lesson plan. Other school districts are not as strict. Make sure that you discuss this with your mentor or other teachers to understand exactly what is required of you as you create your lesson plans.

By allowing states to define their own standards and not mandating national standards, the federal government lets states determine what to teach. For example, Texas social studies standards deal more specifically with state history than Florida social studies standards do. If the national government created standards, this type of individual focus would be impossible to maintain.

On the flip side, if national standards were mandated, proponents claim that curricula would be standardized across the nation. It would become much more likely that the information learned in American history class would not vary from state to state. This issue of state versus national standards will continue to be debated for quite some time.

High-Stakes Testing

Teachers across the nation are increasingly faced with the need to prepare their students for high-stakes testing. For example, at this time all students in Florida must pass the Florida Comprehensive Assessment Test (FCAT) in order to graduate from high school. Further, funding and school grades are based in part on the results of this test.

The goal of tests such as the FCAT is to ensure that students meet minimum levels of achievement at different grades throughout their school careers. There is also a desire to create educational accountability. In a perfect world, teachers would not have to change what they were teaching in order to fully prepare students for tests like the FCAT. However, many times these tests do not mirror the curriculum taught in the classroom. Therefore, teachers spend time preparing the students for the test in addition to covering the curriculum for their courses.

ALERT

As a teacher, you may have to make tough choices concerning your curriculum when you add test preparation into the mix. Just by including additional information, you will have to shorten or remove other topics that you normally would have taught.

Personal Vision

If you do not add your personal educational vision into your lesson plans, you will not be as effective as a teacher. It is important to meet the objectives of the district and state, but you must add your personal stamp to your curriculum to make it real for your students.

Take some time as you create your lessons to determine what you want your students to learn from the material. Settle on the top three to five points you want students to take away from a lesson and make sure you stress these important points while teaching. Write the points you wish to stress on the board or on a handout to help students frame any notes they take.

Make sure that any assessments you create also include these important points. Students will learn what you stress. Conversely, if you spend an inordinate part of your lesson on something that you feel is not that important for your students to learn, you are wasting precious educational time.

Sources of Ideas

Luckily, teachers have many resources to help them create their lessons. In fact, the problem most teachers face is deciding which resources to use. Effective teachers spend some time looking through the available resources and combining many sources to create a personalized lesson. The sources for these ideas include books, the Internet, other teachers, students, and the world around you.

Books and Textbooks

The course textbook is the first source of ideas for lesson plans. However, you're not meant to rely solely on the teacher's edition of your textbook to create your lessons. While these texts often have some excellent resources and ideas, allowing them to form the majority of your lessons will cause you to miss out on some great educational experiences for your students.

Be smart when you use textbooks. Do not simply include a section or a lesson because it is listed in the textbook. Use these as just one tool to create excellent, challenging, and fun lessons.

ALERT

Look at all sources for lessons skeptically. Many textbooks have errors; even if a textbook does not have obvious mistakes, it can still be inaccurate based on the method in which it presents the information. Make sure to read through the entire textbook assignment before you give it to your students.

Many textbook publishing companies also sell additional books and printed materials that will help you create your lesson plans. Here you can find simulations, debates, role-playing scenarios, writing lessons, and other materials that can truly enhance your teaching. Integrating these outside sources into your curriculum can build interest into a possibly boring lesson.

Online Resources

The Internet is also an excellent source of free material for lesson plans. However, it is important to be discerning about the quality of the lessons you find online. Many times, teachers will post lessons they have found effective, but might not work for you and your classroom situation. Therefore, take some time to evaluate the source of your materials, and use common sense to determine if each lesson will really interest your students.

Other Teachers

Rely on other teachers to give you a sense of what does and doesn't work. If other teachers on your staff are teaching the same topic or have taught it in the past, they might have effective lessons that you can use or adapt. Other teachers can also give you practical advice that you may not find elsewhere. Most teachers are very generous about sharing their ideas and materials.

Another way that other teachers can be a real help to new teachers is by giving you another perspective or opinion about lessons you want to try. For example, you could go to a veteran teacher to discuss a new simulation that you are thinking about using. Because of her experience, she can tell you the benefits of the simulation and warn you of potential problems you need to watch out for. Plus, she can give you tips to make teaching the lesson easier.

Students as a Resource

Sometimes students will ask you questions or bring up issues that could form the basis of great lessons. Usually, when students are interested enough in a topic to ask questions about it, you will find that this can provide you with unique opportunities to truly engage them. Further, if they see that you respond to their questions by creating lessons for them, they will be more likely to feel connected and speak up in the future. You can use their ideas to supplement your curriculum. However, you need to use your best judgment here—some topics will be inappropriate or could lead to problems for you in the long run.

The World Around You

Students respond best to ideas that they know well. Therefore, using real-world examples will help students connect to your curriculum. Sources for educational ideas are all around you. Remain aware of the latest trends and ideas, and try to find ways to incorporate them. However, stay away from trying to relate to students "on their level." Most of the time, teachers who try to use the current slang become objects of ridicule.

ESSENTIAL

> Teachers must juggle and combine many sources to create truly unique and interest-building lessons. You can find sources for ideas all around you, so make sure to keep a notebook with you and jot down great ideas as they arise.

Your Planning Tools

You have books, textbooks, the Internet, other teachers, students, and the world around you to help come up with engaging lesson plans. These tools are necessary, but this still leaves a lot of work when it comes to your lesson plans. Planning works best when you start from the general and move toward the specific. For example, determine the themes of your units before creating the individual lessons within the units.

School Calendar

The first step you should take as you start lesson planning is to create a school calendar. You can use an actual calendar, but it might be useful to simply create your own.

Once you have your blank calendar in front of you, mark off all the vacation days. Then, mark off any dates for testing (if you know what they are at this point). If you know an event is going to happen in a month but you are not sure what the date is yet, make a note at the top of that month's calendar page. For example, if you know that homecoming happens during one week in October, mark that down and determine how many days' lessons you are going to lose because of events, assemblies, and so on. If you are teaching a grade with a required high-stakes test, then make sure to note time for test preparation.

When you are done, count up the number of days that you have left. Make sure to subtract for the days that you noted at the top of each month.

This is the maximum number of days you think that you will have to actually teach your students. Now, subtract one more day each month to account for unexpected events that will arise, and you will have a fairly accurate count of what you can expect each month.

Once you have this determined, you can start deciding how many units of study you are going to have in the class and how many days you will need for each unit. To determine the number of days you will need for each unit, you will need to work closely with your texts and other resources to see how much and the type of material you have available. Once you have a tentative time frame worked out, pencil in the starting date for each unit on the calendar. As the year progresses, mark out new days away from class as they arise, and adjust your plan accordingly.

ESSENTIAL

As you plan, it is important to appeal to different learning styles and use different techniques. This is not to say that you must teach to every learning style at every point. However, keep in mind that if you always lecture or always do seatwork, your students will become bored and lose interest.

This calendar will be the foundation for your curriculum. It gives you an overall picture of what you are going to be covering and when. Teachers who do not create calendars often fail to understand why they cannot cover all the necessary material. The calendar allows you to determine if you are on track. You can then adjust lessons to make sure that you meet your curriculum objectives.

Plan Book

Your calendar will work hand in hand with your plan book. The plan book allows you to include more details for each day. In your plan book, you note all of the activities you are going to cover each day in each of your periods. Make sure to start on a new, blank page of the plan book for each unit. Then use your materials and ideas to create a focus for each day.

Knowing How Much to Include

It's tough to know how much to include in a new lesson. While you can gain some insight into timing through years of experience, even veteran teachers occasionally overplan or underprepare. If you have to choose, err on the side of overplanning. It is much easier to cut things out of a plan or continue it on the next day than to fill up twenty minutes. With this said, your goal should be to always plan for about ten minutes longer than you think you will need. Keep a stock of "mini-lessons" that you can pull out as needed in order to fill up any extra time you might have.

Effective Use of Cliffhangers

One technique that effective teachers employ is to use cliffhangers at the end of a day's lesson. When you are excited about your subject, your students will be as well. Leave the kids little hints to entice them; this excitement will carry over to the next day's lesson.

Cliffhangers can take many forms, including handouts, questions on the board, or brief discussions that leave questions unanswered until the next day. Keep the cliffhangers in mind as you create your lessons.

Assigning Homework

Part of lesson planning for most teachers is designing the homework assignments. To avoid creating ineffective assignments, you need to begin by defining your beliefs about the purpose of homework. Assignments should reinforce central ideas and provide students with methods for exhibiting knowledge in unique ways. Whenever possible, make homework connect to real life. Give students the opportunity to practice using the information that you have taught them, so that they can learn to make connections between what they learn and current events or skills that they will use throughout their lives.

When creating homework assignments, give further consideration to the amount of time and effort you wish to put into grading student work. Remember, you will need to grade all the homework you assign. This does not mean that you should avoid important assignments like essays or laboratory reports. However, it does mean that you might think about placing easier-to-grade (not necessarily easier-to-complete) assignments in between those that are more time-consuming.

Homework Concerns

Is homework necessary at all? This question is actually being debated among some educational experts today. Some experts argue that because of students' busy schedules, homework should be seriously reduced or eliminated. Further, numerous studies have shown that, at least in elementary school, there is not much correlation between achievement and the amount of homework that a student completes. Most educators, however, believe that effective, challenging homework assignments are a necessary part of education. By eliminating homework, students eliminate reinforcement. How can you possibly learn your multiplication tables without a lot of outside study?

QUESTION

What is Bloom's taxonomy?
Benjamin Bloom's taxonomy categorizes educational questions according to their level of abstraction: knowledge, comprehension, application, analysis, synthesis, and evaluation. Many teachers do not move much beyond knowledge and comprehension. Effective teachers spend some time moving further along the taxonomy with their students.

Despite the common belief that homework is necessary, when you look at who is actually giving homework, the results can be surprising. Elementary educators appear to give their students the most homework. Middle school teachers also give homework, though often in lesser amounts than elementary school teachers. And high school teachers seem to give the least amount of homework. Teachers of college preparatory/honors classes are the exception to this rule.

The reasons for this trend are varied. First, elementary educators might assign a lot to complete at home, but they are usually assignments on the lower level of Bloom's taxonomy, meant to reinforce important concepts that were taught in class. On the other hand, high school educators should be covering material that challenges students to move up Bloom's taxonomy toward higher-order thinking. Therefore, the quantity of homework should be lessened, but the quality should be increased. Of course, there are some questions about whether the majority of teachers actually do this.

Why else might high school teachers assign less homework? One reason would be pressure from some parents and students. Students today often have jobs and participate in numerous extracurricular activities. They complain that they do not have the time to complete homework every night. Even though teachers might question their priorities, some decide that it is easier to avoid having numerous kids ignore or turn in subpar homework. They shun homework altogether or give assignments that can be completed in class.

One other reason high school students may appear to have less homework is that there seems to be more time in the school day for students to complete work. Students who do have busy lives will take advantage of down moments to complete other assignments. Elementary school children often have their days filled moving from subject to subject. They do not have as much study time or free time at their disposal.

How Much Is Enough?

So how much homework should you give? You should strive to have enough to reinforce and teach the core ideas, but not so much that students have time for little more than homework. This is a fine line to walk.

If you are an elementary school teacher, you know exactly what homework your students have because you are in charge of assigning all work. You can control exactly how long students are working each evening. You decide what your students need and assign accordingly. However, if you have a lot of students with learning disabilities, you will need to adjust the quantity of homework slightly, because an assignment that might take a student without disabilities thirty minutes, could take a student with learning disabilities two hours.

Middle school teachers often work on teams and can join together to control the amount of homework students are assigned. For example, each class could be assigned a homework day. On Mondays, the social studies teacher might give out homework, on Tuesdays, it's the English teacher's turn, and so on. The team could also decide that all teachers give out fifteen-minute assignments each day. The team would schedule any major assignments together.

The real problem lies with high school teachers who do not work in coherent teams and therefore cannot consult with other teachers to control homework for each student. Generally, this does not cause major issues in average classes. However, when students are participating in honors and advanced placement courses, they can run into a real problem with exorbitant amounts of homework.

FACT

According to the U.S. Department of Education, national organizations suggest that students in grades kindergarten to two should receive ten to twenty minutes of homework each school day. In grades three to six, children should spend thirty to sixty minutes a day on homework. In grades seven to nine, students would benefit from more homework time.

If students have to work five or more hours every evening to complete their assignments, then they probably are not getting enough exercise or sleep to be healthy. At the very least, it would be useful for high school teachers to discuss with each other the big assignments they are planning each term to space them out. However, as a new teacher, you will probably find resistance from some veterans to any attempts to alter homework assignments. You will most likely be the one doing the bending and changing.

Learning to Be Flexible

Change is ever-present in education, so it is important that you keep this idea of flexibility in all of your lesson plans. Some courses truly need periods of time without interruption so that important assignments, like science experiments and timed tests, can be completed. Therefore, these assignments must be given on days when you have the least chance of interruption. In other words, do not assign a time-imperative lab on a day when a planned fire alarm is scheduled to occur.

However, be aware that despite all the planning, you will eventually have to face the inevitable and scrap a great lesson because the time was stolen by an unexpected event. In the end, it is important to have a flexible attitude at all times, if for nothing more than your own health.

CHAPTER 9

Maximizing Your Instructional Time

Instructional time is precious. While some days it might seem like the year will never end, if you do the math you will find that your time with students in class is very limited. The attention span of students is such that even long stretches of time are broken up by disruptions, which reduce your effective teaching time. Therefore, it is important to use every minute you have to help students get the best educational experience possible.

Warm-ups

When you are teaching, your goal should be to have students engaged from the moment they walk in your classroom to the moment they leave. While this is never fully possible with every student, it is a worthy goal that will lead to positive choices for you and your students. One way to begin each day on the right foot is to have a warm-up waiting for students as they walk through the door. These can be used in all grades and are useful for preparing students for the day's lessons.

Warm-ups are very short assignments that students complete within the first few minutes of class while you are taking care of important housekeeping tasks like taking attendance. However, they are not limited to just the beginning of class. They can be used in elementary grades to bring students back into focus after returning from lunch or PE. Warm-ups help prepare students for lessons, making it clear that you mean for them to work when they are in your class.

Methods of Use

If used well, warm-ups can give focus to the day's lessons or provide key reviews of the previously learned material. Students are often asked simple questions based on information learned. They can also be required to give short, thoughtful responses that require them to integrate their learning into the real world. One example of a warm-up in a high school economics class might be, "What was one economic choice that you made yesterday? What was your opportunity cost?" Students can quickly answer the questions by relating their life to concepts they have already learned in class. Similarly, an example for an elementary classroom where students have been studying the differences between the earth and the moon might be, "How would life be different on the moon than on earth?"

It is imperative that if you choose to use warm-ups, you do so consistently. Most teachers find that having the warm-up on the board or on an overhead sheet is the best method of presentation, though you might find that some questions work better when printed on a piece of paper.

Grading Warm-ups

Teachers often wonder how to grade these warm-ups. You can choose to collect and grade the warm-ups each day or have the students use a warm-up notebook that they date. You collect these at intervals of your choosing to grade them. The advantage to this is that there are fewer papers to grade each day, leaving time for other important tasks.

ESSENTIAL

Warm-ups are also an effective way to reduce discipline problems at the beginning of class. Students are involved in something academic from the start. They do not have free time to get into trouble.

Some teachers grade students for completion, while others grade for accuracy. These should not be assignments that significantly lower a student's grade if completed poorly, but they should have some consequences so that students stay on task.

If you have used warm-ups correctly, they should relate to and reinforce the work that is going on in class. If you choose to require students to complete all warm-ups in their notebooks, then you should keep your own notebook with all warm-up questions listed. This will help you remember on which days you assigned which questions.

Keeping a Journal

Some teachers find that journal writing is a good way to keep students occupied until class begins. Students keep a notebook that they pull out and write in during the first five minutes of class. The teacher can assign a topic for the day or allow students to write what they want or do a combination of both. Especially in the upper grades, teachers might choose to guide their students' journals to follow the curriculum of the course but then allow them a day of freedom every once in a while where they can just share their thoughts.

The advantage to journal writing is that students get a chance to express themselves about various topics. You can get to know your students a little better through their journals. Journals can provide students with a place to discuss any issues they are having. Sometimes students feel better about asking for help on paper than they do out loud in front of the rest of the class.

Journal writing is also an effective tool for emerging writers. By getting elementary school students to write about their weekend or other interesting topics, they practice this important skill without realizing it. One interesting use of journals beyond the classroom is to send the journal home for extended breaks and ask the students and parents to write to each other in the journal. This helps continue the practice of daily writing and increase parental involvement.

ALERT

If you find evidence of suicidal thoughts, violent tendencies, or abuse at home in your student's journal, you have a responsibility to report this to your administrator and the guidance counselor. They will help you decide the best course of action from there. It is illegal to withhold certain kinds of information, such as evidence of possible child abuse by parents or guardians.

However, journals do pose some problems for teachers. For one thing, they have to be graded. Grading journals takes more time than grading warm-ups. Also, because of the freedom inherent in journal writing, students can sometimes discuss topics that are inappropriate. It is your job to make sure that students know your expectations about their journals. Just because you are allowing students to share their thoughts and opinions does not mean they have the right to write whatever they want.

Housekeeping Time

The beginning of each day usually involves many tasks that you must complete for accounting and educational purposes. Taking attendance, collecting homework, and dealing with students who were absent the previous day are all tasks that can quickly eat up five minutes or more of class time. If you are using warm-ups, five minutes might be acceptable, but not much more because students will quickly get off-task.

Getting a class started after students are off-task can be a difficult and time-consuming endeavor. Therefore, it is important that you come up with efficient methods for dealing with common issues so that you can get down to the real task of teaching quickly.

Taking Attendance

Probably the most important housekeeping task you will have to complete each day is taking attendance and determining absentees. This is important not only for your record-keeping purposes but, more importantly, for legal purposes. If you report a student as absent from your class, you will have no further issue in the matter if he does something illegal. However, if you mark a student as present in your class when he was actually absent or, worse yet, if you have no idea if a student was present or absent on a particular day, you can encounter difficulties from both the administration and the authorities if illegal or dangerous activities occur.

It also is important to have accurate attendance records in the event of emergencies, like a tornado or fire. Otherwise, students who were actually absent from your class, but considered present, may be judged as missing. Most schools require teachers to take their attendance books when they have to leave their classroom for a fire alarm.

ESSENTIAL

Having assigned seats is a real boon to quick attendance-taking. You can simply look down the seating chart and see whose seat is empty. Your goal should be to take only one or two minutes for attendance taking while students are completing their warm-ups.

There's no question that attendance records are important, but they can still be time-consuming to keep unless you have a good system in place. In the beginning of the year, taking attendance out loud can help you reinforce name learning. However, you should strive to take attendance quietly after you have learned your students' names.

In your attendance book, it is a good idea to have different symbols for unexcused absences, excused absences, and tardies. Often, schools have their own method, which you should follow. However, if your school does not have a set method, then you must come up with your own. Try to create a system that is quick to implement and easy to read at a later date.

Collecting Homework

Collecting homework is another necessary task that should be done efficiently, or it will begin eating up a lot of your class time. Teachers have various techniques for collecting homework. If you are teaching in elementary school, you might want to consider having a homework folder that you collect each day. This way, the homework is always in the same place, you can collect it from the folders whenever you get a spare moment without disrupting class, and if parents want to send you a special note they know you will be checking the folder each day.

ALERT

The teachers who have the worst problem with homework are those who walk from student to student collecting the work. This wastes a lot of time and gives students even more time to get off-task. Remember to try and be as efficient as possible to maximize the educational time for your students.

If you are teaching in a situation where students are moving from class to class, then you might decide to collect homework as students walk into your room each period. You stand at the door, and the students learn that they are to have their homework ready before they walk in your class. This minimizes the time necessary to complete this task.

An alternative is to have a "homework box" that is only available to students before class begins. Students must turn in their homework before the time you designate, or it is considered late. However, understand that you will need to be flexible for students with good excuses, so you might consider including the first three minutes after class begins as additional turn-in time.

It is not a good idea to accept homework at the end of a period. Students will quickly catch on to your habit and will work on their homework in class instead of listening to you. It is best to collect homework at the beginning of the period and assign homework at the end.

Other Common Tasks

You will also be faced with some other common housekeeping tasks throughout the school year. You will have students who need make-up work for absences. As discussed in Chapter 4, you should have an assignment book that students can access during the first few minutes of class to write down their assignments. If you presented notes, you can either make photocopies of overheads, or you can tell students that they need to copy someone else's notes.

Another frequent task is collecting money and/or permission slips. If you are collecting money, you should set up a designated time; the last few minutes of class is best. That way, you have already completed your lesson, and students who are not turning in money can begin working on homework if they wish.

Daily Review

Reviews are a necessary part of education. All people, not just students, need repetition and review to truly learn something new. Students only retain a small portion of what they learn in a classroom each day, so frequent reviews of material are necessary.

At the Beginning of the Class

Most teachers spend a few moments reviewing the previous day's lessons before heading off into new territory. This helps students make connections from day to day and shows them the framework for learning and building on previous knowledge. Warm-ups can help begin this review. After students complete their warm-up, and you have completed your necessary housekeeping tasks, you can move right into review.

You only need to spend a few minutes going over the key points in review. At this time, it is best if you question your students and allow them to show you their knowledge. That can help you clear up any errors they might have in their thinking and allow you to judge the effectiveness of the previous day's lesson. This review should easily transition into the day's lessons.

At the End of the Class

Fewer teachers use an end-of-the-class review. However, this is a very effective tool that teachers should employ more often. Basically, before the students leave for the day, spend a few minutes with your students going over the key points they should take away from what they have learned. This can help you catch errors early before they go home and complete the assigned readings or homework on the same topic.

End-of-the-class review also helps students leave understanding exactly what you wanted them to learn from a lesson. It is most effective when you have completed an alternative learning activity, like a role-play or simulation. Often the educational purpose of these types of lessons can be lost in the fun of the experience. By bringing students back to the reality of the classroom through review, you can reinforce key points. End-of-the-class review is an effective way to emphasize important topics and provide students with a focus for any homework assignments.

QUESTION

How long does short-term memory last without repetition?
According to human-memory research, memories only last about twenty to thirty seconds, unless they are repeated and rehearsed. The more time you can spend on reviewing a subject, the more likely students are to retain and move the information into long-term memory.

Moving from Activity to Activity

Learning to move smoothly from one activity to another is an essential teaching skill. In elementary school classrooms, multiple activities fill each day. Most teachers will post a schedule showing students when they will move from one activity to the next. For example, an elementary activity schedule might contain the following:

8:30–8:55 — Student Warm-Up/Journal Writing
8:55–9:55 — Reading
10:00–10:45 — Specials

10:50–12:20 — Math
12:25–1:00 — Lunch
1:05–1:55 — Writing
2:00–2:30 — Independent Reading/Projects
2:35–3:05 — Social Studies/Science (Mon.–Thurs.)
2:35–3:05 — Recess (Fri.)
3:10 — Cleanup and Review
3:20 — Dismissal

However, even though they might be with students for shorter periods of time, most middle and high school teachers will also find that they have students complete multiple tasks each day. For example, let's say you have the following tasks planned for a single high school class period:

1. Students complete a warm-up while you take roll (three minutes).
2. You review the previous day's lesson (three minutes).
3. Students take a five-question quiz about their reading from the night before (eight minutes).
4. You hold a whole-group discussion about the reading from the night before (ten minutes).
5. You break the class up into small groups and assign them each a character from the reading for whom they are to write a brief biography (twenty minutes).
6. You get the class back together, spend time reviewing, and assign homework before dismissal (six minutes).

As you look through this list of activities, you will see that there are many transitions between one activity and another. Your goal is to make these transitions seamless, wasting as little time as possible. The first step toward this goal is getting organized.

Get Organized

Organization can seem difficult at first because it requires some discipline on your part. However, if you are not organized, you will waste time looking for items or determining what's next in your lesson. For example, if you are giving a quiz and you don't have them easily accessible, then your students will probably get off-task as you look for them.

You should teach students that at the end of assignments and tests they complete in class, they are always to pass their papers to the front so you can collect them. Think in terms of efficiency for yourself and your students.

You can also make transitions easier by guiding students and practicing them early in the year. This is especially true in elementary classrooms. Reinforce the transitions from one subject to another each day until students have it down. For example, if they are to always put their math books on the shelf at the end of the math lesson and then move to the reading circle, make a big deal about this each day until students know exactly what is expected of them. Your goal is to have a quiet and quick transition in order to keep talking and distractions down to a minimum.

Additional Tips and Ideas

Ultimately, maximizing class time is up to you. If you approach each day with the attitude that students will learn in your classroom and that the information you have to teach is important, you will have your priorities straight. Students will pick up on this attitude and realize that they cannot goof off in your class. Of course, this only works if you have an effective, consistent, and enforced discipline plan in place (as described in Chapter 5).

Start Class on Time

Class should begin the moment the bell rings or, in the case of elementary schools, when the students return from lunch, PE, or other activities. Designate your wall clock as the official time for your class to start and stick to it consistently. If you have students learn from the beginning that they are to come in, begin the warm-up, and prepare for the class ahead, you will have won a major battle. This attitude should begin on the very first day of school. Do not be afraid to jump right in and begin teaching that first day. You do not have to do much, but setting the tone of expectations will teach students that they need to pay attention if they wish to pass your class.

Stay Organized

You can work on your own and your students' organization at the same time by creating a posted daily agenda. Having the students copy their agenda into a calendar as explained in Chapter 7 requires students to pay attention to the agenda for the day. Students benefit because they know what to expect and where they are in a lesson. An additional idea is to have students copy these in their daily planners and send them home for signatures at the end of each week. Parents will stay involved and know what their children are learning about in class.

You also will benefit from an agenda. Yours can be as simple as that presented to your students, or it may include other information, like a short list of reminders to yourself. It is easy to lose your place, so having this visual reminder in front of you can help. Some teachers include times on their personal agenda so they can keep the class moving through the day's lesson.

Stay in Control

If you lose control of your class as you deal with disruptions, you will find that it takes a long time for students to get back on task. Some might never get back on task, and you could lose the rhythm of the lesson. Therefore, it is important to keep disruptions to a minimum.

ESSENTIAL

If you have a class in which you often have disruptions, have referrals with you as you teach. Some teachers even go so far as to have a referral filled out. All they have to do is add the student's name if a disruption occurs. This can reduce the time you have to spend on classroom disruptions.

If students are talking or passing notes, call on them to answer questions. This is a subtle way to get them back on task. Writing students' names on the board can be effective for younger students. However, realize that some students might try to argue with you about having their name displayed on the board. Do not engage in this type of verbal sparring in front of your class. Instead, tell the student to discuss it with you after class.

If You Have Extra Time

Despite all of your overplanning and use of reviews, you will sometimes be faced with an extra five to ten minutes. What do you do with this time? Some teachers allow students to simply work on their homework or even chat with their friends. However, with the belief that time is precious, you might want to consider creating some mini-lessons to fill up this time.

Short lessons do not necessarily have to relate to the topic you are currently teaching. You might have a newspaper with you each day in case downtime arises, and you can discuss topics in the news. There are articles in the newspaper that any teacher could use in class. Math teachers can discuss the use and abuse of statistics, science teachers can look at the technology section of newspapers to get great topics of discussion, and English teachers can have students analyze grammar. In fact, one of the best places for students to look for the use of an extensive vocabulary is on the sports page. And the list goes on.

Another idea is to invest in some educational puzzle books. It is fun to pull out "lateral-thinking puzzles" and have students work together to come up with the answer. Similarly, you might pull out trivia questions and have students quickly compete in teams. You could keep a running tab over time of which team is in the lead throughout the year.

The leftover minutes in a period are a great time to get students to really think. They can also build interest in your class. Students are allowed to have a little more fun than usual. Think before you allow these moments to be wasted by letting students talk among themselves or allowing them to fall asleep.

CHAPTER 10

A Variety of Teaching Methods

Teachers often feel they are expected to teach to all levels of students using all learning styles at all times. This is a losing proposition. It will result in your becoming stressed and less effective as a teacher. Instead of trying to be all things to all people, focus on varying your instruction. One of the myths of learning styles and multiple intelligences is that students can only learn from one particular teaching style. In reality, students should be exposed to different methods to help strengthen their weaker areas.

Three Types of Learning Styles

There are three major types of learners: visual, auditory, and tactile/ kinesthetic. Each person has a learning style that is best for his intake and comprehension of new information. Visual learners generally think in terms of pictures and learn best from visuals and handouts. Auditory learners learn best by listening. They usually like lecture and classroom discussions, and they might need to read written material aloud in order to fully understand it. Tactile/kinesthetic learners learn through touching, feeling, and experiencing the world around them. They do well with hands-on experiments, but they may have a hard time sitting through lectures and notes.

FACT

A visual learner is someone who needs to see a word written down to remember it. An auditory learner would remember a word better by hearing it or saying it out loud. A tactile/kinesthetic learner would probably choose to write down the word in order to learn it best.

Many people have a single learning style that works best for them. However, unless you are physically disabled, you can actually learn through all three learning styles.

Effective Use of Learning Styles

As a teacher, you will find that many of your students are best at tactile/ kinesthetic learning. Because traditional classroom teaching techniques often target visual and auditory learning styles, these students get bored and have trouble concentrating.

It can be hard to incorporate tactile/kinesthetic learning all of the time. Don't try to force the issue, but whenever possible, look for lessons that lend themselves to this type of learning. For example, simulations and role-playing allows students to get more hands-on and actually experience what they are learning.

Ineffective Use of Learning Styles

As you consider your students' dominant learning styles, don't go overboard and assume that they cannot learn in other ways. While other styles might be more difficult for them, your students should learn to adapt to all types of instruction. You can help them prepare for less sympathetic teachers by showing them techniques they can use to enhance their learning through each type of style.

Nine Measures of Intelligence

The theory of multiple intelligences, as devised by Howard Gardner, proposes that the traditional intelligence quotient (IQ) measure of intelligence does not illuminate the whole or even a significant part of the overall picture. According to Gardner, there are nine multiple intelligences, and each person has her own strengths and weaknesses:

1. Linguistic intelligence
2. Logical-mathematical intelligence
3. Spatial intelligence
4. Bodily kinesthetic intelligence
5. Musical intelligence
6. Interpersonal intelligence
7. Intrapersonal intelligence
8. Naturalist intelligence
9. Existential intelligence

Gardner's theory has had a huge impact on education. Educators are moving toward a more holistic approach to intelligence and education. This kid-centered idea is an excellent starting point for teachers. However, teachers need to be clear on what are appropriate uses of this theory.

Effective Use of Multiple Intelligences

Teachers tend to focus their instruction on the first two types of intelligence: linguistic and logical-mathematical. However, many students are not strong in both or even one of these areas. As you design your lessons, you need to keep this in mind and adjust your plans to help all students achieve at their highest level.

Adjusting lesson plans does not mean that you need to meet all of the multiple intelligences in all lessons. It does mean that you should provide some variety in your instruction. When you are faced with a new unit, try to think of ways that you can add some interest-building activities that rely on the less-frequently used types of intelligence. For example, in a social studies class studying the 1960s, you could introduce some protest music for discussion to appeal to your students' musical intelligence.

Develop All Types of Intelligence

Many students are not strong in the linguistic form of intelligence. However, students will probably meet many teachers at all levels who will lecture to them and possibly provide them with notes written on an overhead or the board. You need to help students learn strategies for strengthening their linguistic intelligence.

ESSENTIAL

Students need the confidence to succeed. Those who have problems with lectures and notes often lack confidence in their abilities. They do not try for fear of failing. Help build confidence by scaffolding notes and lectures for your students.

For younger students, simply reading books aloud while you check for comprehension can help build this skill. From middle school on, you can teach students how to take notes from oral lectures by providing them with your own notes in the beginning and eventually weaning them away from these with less and less information. Further, teach students how to summarize information that they have read in order to better understand what is important. Developing students' multiple types of intelligence is the best way to prepare them for the future.

Importance of Varying Instruction

As you can see, varied instruction is not only desirable—it is a necessity. Varying instruction means that you do not just rely on one means of teaching students the material. Teachers who rely too much on role-playing and cooperative learning are committing just as great of an error as those who focus on lecture.

Varying instruction is important because it helps build interest in your class. Even if you have a student who works best when given an assignment to read from a book and answer questions, he will enjoy and benefit from other forms of learning.

FACT

In 1956, Benjamin Bloom found that over 95 percent of test questions that students encountered only required them to think at the lowest level: the recall of knowledge. It is imperative that you choose to ask questions at higher levels in order to help students think critically.

Varying instruction can also help you move your teaching beyond the lower levels of Bloom's taxonomy. Incorporating critical thinking skills into your lessons is easier when you are varying the way you present the material. Although you cannot teach students to recall information like multiplication tables with this instruction, you can teach them to analyze and synythesize information.

Class Lectures

Lecturing is a common method for delivering a lot of material to students. In a lecture, the teacher stands in front of the room and explains the material. While you should not lecture to your students every day, there is a time and a place for a lecture, especially in the upper grades. Lectures will often provide students with the greatest amount of material in the shortest amount of time. Further, helping students work on taking notes during lectures will give them an important skill for their future educational careers.

Issues to Consider

Many education professionals claim that lecture is not an effective form of instruction. They argue that it does not engage the students in the learning process because students are passive during the lecture while the teacher is active. Some educational professionals go so far as to say there is never a good time for lecture. However, this can be a disservice to students, especially those who are preparing for college. They will have many college professors who will do nothing but lecture. Therefore, when you decide that a lecture is the best method for a particular lesson, be sure to help your students by providing verbal clues and teaching them note-taking techniques.

You will definitely want to consider the make up of students in your class when deciding whether to lecture. If you have a lot of learning-disabled students in your class who would have a hard time listening and taking notes at the same time, you might want to provide them with a written form of your lecture. Some teachers give students a written outline at the beginning of the lecture so that students can then add further information to the outline during the lecture. Other teachers wait until the end or only give the outlines to students with learning disabilities.

Helping Students with Lectures

Note taking can be a difficult task for many students. Therefore, it is important that educators help students learn how to take notes. Many students have problems understanding how to take notes because they cannot discern what is and what is not important. Therefore, when you are first teaching your students how to listen to lectures, it is important to teach them verbal cues that teachers often use to inform students that an important point has been made.

One example of a verbal clue is repetition. If you repeat a point two or three times, students should realize that it is important and is something they need to write down and remember. Similarly, if you write words and points down on the board or overhead as you are talking, students will realize that they too need to be jotting down the information. You can be even more overt and make a statement before each really important piece of information that lets the students know they need to remember what you are about to say.

Group Discussions

An alternative to straight lecture is class discussion. Instead of the teacher simply telling the students the material with only occasional questions, whole-group discussions are more interactive. The teacher will still present some new material but the students will be required to participate by answering questions and providing examples. This has the advantage of involving students much more in the learning process. Further, it can be used effectively with younger students for short periods of time. However, unless you require participation and use a system to mark each student who speaks, it can be hard to get everyone involved.

Breaking up the class into smaller groups of four to six students is another alternative for older students. Each group then receives a topic of discussion and questions they need to answer as a group. The teacher is much further removed from this type of discussion, which can have both positive and negative effects. As long as each group remains on task, holding small group discussions can be very rewarding.

ALERT

Some students find joy in bringing up inappropriate topics for discussion. Be conscious of your students and try to see where they are heading with comments so that you can quickly intervene if the discussion seems to be moving in an inappropriate direction.

Rules for Discussion

It is important that you set up some ground rules for your students to follow during group discussions. A good rule is that during the class discussion, only one person should be talking at a time. You need to make it clear to your students that they are not to make fun of each other for their opinions. In a healthy discussion, it's normal for people to disagree, and your students need to learn how to respect their peers' opinions.

It is your job to act as the facilitator and keep the discussion on topic. You may be faced with students who have a different agenda and try to move the discussion to irrelevant topics. Their comments may even be of some educational value—for instance, they may relate to current events. However, unless a comment is something that needs to be discussed or is a teachable moment, you should not deviate from your original lesson plan.

Guiding the Discussion

One of the most important skills in your teaching arsenal is the ability to question effectively. Most teachers make the mistake of asking a question, waiting about three seconds, and then providing the answer. However, wait time is one of the most important components of effective questioning.

It is difficult to get the knack of how long to pause after asking a question. At first, it will feel as if you are waiting too long. However, waiting will get students to answer your questions. Your students will begin to realize that you are going to wait for them to raise their hands and respond. This does not mean that you should wait for a minute after each question; waiting ten seconds should be long enough.

The other major pitfall is the use of multiple questions. For example, the following is an improper question to ask students: "What is the largest river in the world? Where is it located? How long is it?" This type of question causes problems for several reasons. For one thing, students will have a hard time remembering all the parts of the question. Secondly, they may not want to speak up if they do not know all of the answers. Finally, students may become confused about the correct answer for any of the questions or, worse, lose sight of what is really the point of the lesson.

It is also important to review how you respond to student answers. If you try to find something worthwhile in what a student says, even if she is wrong, then you will encourage her to answer again in the future. For example, which of the following responses is more encouraging? "That is wrong, Sarah," or "You are right that this was written in the Enlightenment period, but you have not given the correct author for the piece." Obviously, the second provides more information and also allows the student to see that she was partially correct.

Learning Centers

Learning centers are an effective form of instruction in the elementary grades. The room is set up into centers where students can participate in a variety of activities. Then students are given the opportunity to complete activities either of their own choosing or with teacher direction at these centers.

Typically, a teacher will set up his room in a traditional manner with an art center, a library/reading center, a computer center, a science center, and so on. Each day, students are given the opportunity to go to the center of their choice and choose what they wish to do. The teacher might set out new manipulatives or place books out based on the theme that is being taught.

A great way to extend learning centers is to provide students with guided work. The students can select the order in which they wish to visit each center, but by the end of a week, for example, they have to complete an activity at each one. For example, say you are teaching a unit on plants; you could set up centers as follows:

Science Center—Students grow their own rye seed.
Arts Center—Students use leaves to create a picture.
Writing Center—Students write a story about planting a garden.
Poetry Center—Students memorize a poem about plants or gardening.
Reading Center—Students read a book such as *The Tiny Seed* by Eric Carle.

Using centers in this manner requires a lot of organization and planning on the part of the teacher. However, these centers are beneficial because students are staying active, learning by means of varying activities, and working at their own pace, yet they are still required to produce results that are assessed when the unit is completed.

Cooperative Learning

Cooperative learning is the practice of placing students into groups and having them work together to complete assignments. If you ask ten different teachers their opinions about cooperative learning, you will find a wide variety of answers. Some teachers rely on it heavily, while others barely—if ever—use it.

The fact is that effective cooperative learning takes a lot of time on the teacher's part. It is quite easy to get students into groups and have them complete a worksheet together. However, this is not true cooperative learning. Instead, students need to be given roles to fulfill in their group. The information presented must be interesting and challenging at the same time.

Overuse of cooperative learning can lead to boredom and issues between students. Most people have experienced working in a group where one or more members refuse to do anything. Unfortunately, in cooperative learning many teachers have a difficult time differentiating between students within a group. Instead, they just give the entire group the same grade regardless of whether only one person did the work or all of the students contributed. On the other hand, if teachers do try to differentiate between students, this can lead to hard feelings and further problems.

FACT

In the business world, being an effective team member is a necessary skill for advancement. Companies look for people who can effectively work in a cooperative environment. Effective cooperative-learning activities in the classroom can help teach students the important components of teamwork.

Tips and Techniques

So how do you effectively use cooperative learning? As previously stated, you should give each student a role to fulfill in the group. Each role should contribute a part of the overall project. This will help students understand what they should be doing and it helps you divvy out the grades at the end of the lesson.

You should also provide students with a means for presenting their feelings about the efforts of each team member. You might pass out a form that asks each student to rate her own and her team members' work; each student would complete this form privately. If numerous members of a team agree that someone did not participate in the group, this can be combined with your own observations to determine grades.

It is also important to keep cooperative learning groups on task. Divide your cooperative-learning lesson into chunks and tell your students when they should be moving to the next part of the lesson. Also, make sure to circulate through the room and directly observe what each group is doing.

Role-Playing and Debates

Role-playing and debates can be highly effective forms of teaching. When students participate in these types of activities, they are fully engaged. In role-playing, students pretend to be other people and interact as these new persons. In debates, students argue two or more sides of an issue by bringing up facts and important points. If used correctly, these methods can create educational memories that will last a lifetime.

Controlling the Situation

Role-playing and debates can get out of hand if you as a teacher are not in control. You need to have strict rules for each of the activities, and you must enforce them fairly and consistently. When students begin talking at the same time or making fun of each other, you need to stop them immediately.

ALERT

Role-playing puts students in a vulnerable position in which they may be open to ridicule. It is important that you stress proper respect and treatment for those students participating. Even one incident can cause students to avoid participating in future role-playing activities.

Tips and Techniques

It can be challenging to have all students participate in some activities. For example, having a debate with fifteen students on each side is unmanageable. A great technique for debates is to create teams of four or five students each and then have the rest of the class be the audience. Because the debating team has to do a lot of research and work before and during the debate, you need to make sure that the audience does a comparable amount of work.

Therefore, you should require audience members to also do some research before the debate begins and come up with questions that they wish to ask the debating teams at the conclusion of the debate. You could have them take notes during the debate. Finally, you could have these students "judge" which side won the debate.

Role-playing requires a lot of preparation on the part of the teacher before the activity even begins. You must have a clear purpose and understanding of what you wish to accomplish through this technique. If the students are to take on the role of historical figures, they should be responsible for studying that person. You may ask them to research their historical figure, or you may choose to provide them with clues to help them make the characters more realistic. You can even offer extra credit to those who bring costumes.

When a role-playing lesson is finished, students need to be debriefed. There are several methods for debriefing students. You can have them create a reflection journal or answer questions stressing the information you feel was most important. Sometimes, students will really enjoy role-playing and even debating, but they will not necessarily understand what information they need to remember for future exams. End-of-the-lesson review can be very effective at focusing student learning.

CHAPTER 11

Technology in the Classroom

Some schools put a lot of emphasis on technology; others may be unable to come up with the funds necessary to purchase computer hardware and software. Technology, at times, has been viewed as the savior of public education. However, technology is not a solution in and of itself. Presented or used improperly, technology in the classroom may prove to be ineffective, a costly way of wasting valuable teaching time.

The Haves and the Have-Nots

The technological disparity among schools and districts is staggering. Some school districts provide a great deal of funds to buy technology for schools. Many schools across the country are wired for broadband technology, which provides them with high-speed access to the Internet. However, there are also many school districts that do not have enough funds to provide more than a handful of computers to their schools. This disparity only exacerbates the problems in education. In fact, it can often act as a lightning rod for criticism.

The sad fact is that many of the schools that do not have a lot of technology are located in the poorest areas. Since computers and technology have become such an integral part of the world, it is imperative that we do not create a situation where some students are left behind because of where they live. With this said, it is also important that we do not rob important programs like the arts for the funds to purchase additional technology.

It's Not Just about Money

Even though many schools have plenty of technological resources available for their teachers and students, this does not necessarily correlate with increased use and effectiveness in teaching. In fact, one of the main problems that schools have is the way that they or their school districts order and purchase technology. Further, if the school district does not provide teachers with ample time for training, the sad truth is that most teachers will not even use the expensive equipment that has been bought for their and their students' use.

Problem with Technology Purchases

Many schools do not spend enough time researching or planning their technology purchases. They often lack an overall plan for technology, and there is a belief that buying any technology is better than having no technology at all. They often end up purchasing items that are a "good deal" but that might not really be useful in the classroom. Sometimes, these purchases are just too difficult to integrate, or are incompatible with systems already in place.

What schools need is a well-thought-out plan for buying new technology. Teachers should be an integral part of the planning process. Because many new teachers know more about the available technology than veteran teachers, it may be a good idea for you to join the technology committee. By helping to develop a workable purchasing plan, you'll make sure you have the technological tools that will make your teaching experience more efficient and effective.

ALERT

Schools often receive funds from government agencies with strings attached, such as time limits within which to spend the money. This creates the "spend it or lose it" attitude that often leads to unwise technology purchases.

Why Teachers Do Not Use Technology

In many schools across the nation, teachers are presented with a wide array of technological tools. However, many teachers do not use most or even any of this technology. Why not? The answer is not a simple one.

First, teachers lack training in new technology. Some are just shown a brief demo, while others receive no training at all. Teachers who are provided with enough training to become proficient often lack the time to integrate the new systems into their lesson plans. In fact, the majority of teachers feel that integrating technology would be a great way to connect to students, and they wish they had more planning time.

In other instances, the technology provided is just not that useful. Just because a CD-ROM game exists that helps teach a foreign language does not mean that it's a resource easily integrated into a lesson for a group of thirty students.

Is Technology the Answer?

An important question that all schools need to answer is, "What is the purpose of technology in our school?" Will technology solve the major problems facing the school? Will it raise student achievement levels? What impact will it have?

The truth is that technology is not the panacea for all of education's ills. It is simply a tool that effective teachers can use to help reinforce and teach important concepts. It is not the end of education—it is just the beginning.

If teachers rely too heavily on technology without a clear picture of how it should be integrated into their lessons, students may miss out on important parts of the educational process. If a teacher simply sends students to the computer lab each day to work on a computer program, she is not truly teaching. While some programs do provide accountability measures, most do not.

ESSENTIAL

Realize that it takes time for your lesson plans to evolve to include cutting-edge technology. Set a goal to upgrade just a few lessons each year, and you will eventually have a fully integrated classroom.

Even in the case of online courses, experience has shown that a teacher must be an integral part of the educational process for the courses to reach their full potential. (A more in-depth look at online learning can be found in Chapter 21.) Similarly, teachers who simply use technology without trying to determine the best method of use within the framework of their class will not see many benefits.

A Multitude of Resources at Your Disposal

Teachers have a wealth of technology available to them. All they need is the money to purchase these products. In fact, the number of computer games, simulations, and programs available is so great in many curriculum areas that teachers have the ability to be fairly selective before they purchase. Once again, a little bit of research and planning goes a long way toward saving money and buying only what you need and plan to use.

Computer Technology

Many excellent computer games, simulations, and programs exist to support education in the classroom. Manufacturers usually have demonstrations that allow you to get a feel for these programs before ordering them. Realize that when you buy a single copy of a software program, it is meant for personal use. If you plan on using a program with a whole class, your school needs to purchase it for each student or buy a site license that allows unlimited use of a program.

Logistics of setting up programs can often be problematic for teachers. Some schools provide computer labs that teachers can reserve in advance. This allows each student to have access to a computer. If your school does not have enough computers at the computer lab, then you might have to assign groups of students to share computers. You might also need to space out the use of the program over several days, which often results in lost classroom time for other projects and lessons.

ESSENTIAL

Student participation is important when using computer simulations. When you are presenting information through a computer simulation, you might not have the ability to closely monitor student participation. Therefore, create questions and projects for students to complete that require their full attention.

It's Still School

It is also important that you determine a method for assessing students. While many programs are fun, make sure that you verify their educational value before allowing students to use them for assignments. Some computer simulations and games may have good educational potential. However, they might also contain inappropriate violence or humor. Therefore, consider the entire game before including it in your lessons.

Any method of assessment you devise must take into account how much the students can complete in the time allotted. Remember, some students will take more time reading and completing tasks than others. With that said, you must keep a close watch on students to make sure they are truly working and not just goofing off.

Overhead Projectors

Another item that you will probably hear about or have access to is a system that allows you to project the image on your computer monitor to an overhead screen. That way, you can run a program allowing the students to watch and participate. For instance, you could run a historical simulation game in a social studies class, allowing the students to participate in the decision-making process.

Macs and PCs

Most schools today have a lot of Apple and very few—if any—IBM-compatible personal computers (PCs). This has happened over time because Apple has done a great job of providing monetary incentives to schools to purchase their equipment. You must realize that many students will have PCs at home and may not be familiar with Macs. Further, some computer programs are only made for PCs, so check the requirements of your software carefully before purchasing it.

Wireless Labs

Some schools are lucky enough to own wireless labs—class sets of laptop computers linked to a central computer that you control. If your school is wired for broadband technology, then your students can access the Internet and do research from their own desks. You can monitor what students are doing while providing them with a new way to approach education.

Learning Online

The rise of the Internet has changed many different parts of life, from shopping to education. Students are turning more and more frequently to the Internet for research. Quality online education has been on the rise with organizations like the Florida Virtual School. You can even find excellent programs like virtual field trips on the Internet. These activities take your students through quality websites and ask them questions about the information they find. However, there are many issues and problems associated with the Internet that you and your students need to be aware of.

Offensive Sites

One of the foremost concerns of many parents is what their children are accessing on the Internet. Some schools place restrictive software on their computers to limit the types of sites that students can visit. However, this is not always the best solution because both offensive and inoffensive sites can be blocked. Further, there are some legal questions concerning their constitutionality in terms of free speech.

FACT

Approximately 220 million people were online in the United States during June 2008. This accounts for over 72 percent of the U.S. population. Since 2000, this number has grown by over 129 percent and will only continue to grow over time.

Conversely, if your school does not have this type of software on its computers, students can access any site. Therefore, schools usually have strict acceptable-use policies concerning what students and teachers can access on the Internet. Students who are caught accessing pornographic or otherwise offensive sites are subject to punishment. It is important to remember that if students access these types of sites during your class, you may be called to answer questions from parents or administrators. Therefore, do your best to make sure that students are working appropriately.

Online Information May Be Wrong or Misleading

Another issue that often arises with the use of the Internet is the quality of the information that is accessed. While there is a lot of excellent information available, there is also a lot of inaccurate and potentially dangerous material accessible to students. It is very important that you and your students learn to discriminate between good and bad sites.

It is also important that students realize that all people write with a certain amount of prejudice, based on their beliefs. Therefore, if students are citing an article about global warming, they need to be aware that the author most probably has personal beliefs about the situation. If they looked elsewhere, they would probably find contrary opinions. When evaluating websites, you and your students will want to ask the following questions:

- Is the author listed, and can you read his or her biographical information?
- Is the website associated with a product or sponsored by a particular interest group?
- Is the information dated? Does it say when the site was last updated?
- Does the author cite any resources?

It is also a good idea to have students compare any unique or controversial data with more established print publications. The quality of the sources that students use should be an integral part of the grading process.

ESSENTIAL

Critical analysis of all sources of information, not just Internet sites, is an important skill that students should learn. Just because something is in print or is on the evening news does not mean that it is entirely accurate or without bias.

Using Technology Effectively

In order to effectively and seamlessly integrate technology into your classroom, you must be very familiar with its operation. Do not present a computer program to students that you have not practiced using first. You should know the ins and outs of the program, so that when students run into problems you have the answers ready. Without this initial experience, technology will always be awkward and will take more time than it is worth.

You should also have an alternative lesson ready whenever you use technology, in case there's a glitch. If you are using the Internet, your connection might be down. If you are using a computer program, something could have happened to corrupt the disk. In other words, make sure that you are prepared in case the worst scenario happens. Do not lose precious teaching time by failing to have another lesson prepared.

ALERT

Veteran teachers are often resistant to innovations and new technology. As a newer teacher, you will find that some teachers might discount your innovative ideas as not workable. If you believe in the integration of technology, do not allow their negative attitudes to stop you from trying new resources.

There are many activities that you can do with the technology that is available today. Research, for example, has been made so much richer with the advent of the Internet. It used to be that students were limited to the books and periodicals available at their school or local libraries. Now they have many more options available to them. Further, programs such as the World Book and Grolier's that are available on CD-ROM can provide interactive experiences to help enhance traditional encyclopedias and textbooks.

When Your School Can't Afford It

Not all schools can afford to purchase the most up-to-date technology. In fact, some schools are lucky to have a small number of computers. Students and teachers at these schools lose out on a number of highly effective programs and devices to aid in learning. Without having to dig deep into your own pockets, how can you bring this technology into your school?

Government and Private Grants

Government agencies and private industries often advertise technology grants available to teachers and schools. Grant writing is a special art that requires patience, so it is a good idea to do some research into effective grant-writing techniques before you start applying for these types of grants. Remember, when you apply for a grant, you include a proposal for how the award will be used. If you are awarded the grant, you must show your progress toward your stated goal, which requires record keeping and further effort on your part.

Other Alternatives

You can also try a more grassroots effort for buying technology. Why not organize a fundraiser to buy software programs or computers? If you are teaching in a high school, you could have service organizations at your school participate and win awards for the most money raised.

Visit local businesses and try to get them to sponsor classrooms. They may be willing to aid in the purchase of computers or programs. Then you could have the school newspaper recognize their contribution. If you can get the community behind your effort, then technology can become an integral part of your educational strategy.

CHAPTER 12

Assessments and Grading

Effective lessons need to be accompanied by authentic assessments—evaluations or tests that directly examine what students have learned. When students have successfully completed an authentic assessment, the teacher can feel confident that they have learned the major topics and ideas presented in the lessons. It takes a lot of work to create effective, authentic assessments and to grade them in a fair and consistent fashion.

Valid Assessments

Assessments should measure what you teach to your students. That might sound simplistic, but many times teachers who believe they have created valid assessments are disappointed with the results. For example, if your assignment questions or directions are confusing, then you might not get the results you expect.

Try to read through your questions from a student's point of view to catch and clarify any confusing points before you give a quiz or assignment. If the results of an evaluation are still not as expected, do not be afraid to evaluate your assessment for validity. If you find that it was at fault, you could have the students complete a new assessment. Over time, you will get a real feel for what students will respond to and what will confuse them.

Norm-Referenced Assessments

There are two ways of grading assessments. Norm-referenced assessments compare the scores of students against others who have already taken the same tests. These are used most typically for standardized tests like the SAT. Students are compared to a reference group to determine how they rank. Usually, the focus of norm-referenced tests is to discriminate between students rather than to determine mastery of a body of knowledge.

Criterion-Referenced Assessments

Criterion-referenced assessments measure how well students have learned the material. This is the most common type of assessment used by teachers in the classroom. It is possible for everyone to earn a passing grade, as long as they have learned the information.

Pretesting to Track Progress

Teachers do not need to give assessments only after teaching a lesson. In fact, it can often be useful to test students before a lesson in order to determine their understanding of the subject. For example, if you are reviewing basic addition facts in second grade, assessing students first can help you find any weak points students might have. Additionally, teachers of language arts can give spelling pre-tests. They can then use the results to determine if a student should continue to study the regular spelling list or be given a new "challenge" list.

Pre-tests can also give you a basis for determining how much students actually master from your classroom activities. You can see if they have increased in knowledge and understanding when compared to post-tests. Some teachers even base their students' grades on the amount of increase between the pre- and post-tests.

ESSENTIAL

Measurement and evaluation is probably the most valuable of all courses offered in colleges of education. This is because creating valid tests is a difficult proposition. Make sure that you review the information you learned there and avoid common pitfalls of test creation.

If you follow this route, make sure you avoid using exactly the same questions on both tests. Students will eventually catch on that they can simply study exactly what was asked on the first test to do well on the second one. However, you should blend some of the same questions in with new ones to measure improvement and achievement. You should use your own observations of student achievement and progression in combination with the results from these tests. This is a common practice used in the elementary school setting and should be included in middle and high school.

What Do Grades Really Mean?

What is the purpose and meaning of grades? What is the difference in your mind between an A and a B or an E and an S? Should top grades be given only for mastering hard-to-learn concepts or information? You really need to look at these and many other questions before you begin grading students.

There has been some controversy about whether grading is a good or even appropriate practice. Some people question the overall effect of grading on the self-esteem of the student. However, at this point grading and assessments remain one of the few ways we have to determine mastery of knowledge.

Elementary School Grades

Teachers and many parents approach grades differently in elementary school than they do in middle and high schools. In one way, this approach is very healthy. Teachers are able to provide parents with an understanding of where their student stands based on the required benchmarks for that grade. Then the parents and teachers can use this information to provide better instruction and help to the student.

If a student earns all E's except for one S in reading, the parents should understand that the student might need a little extra help in that subject. Obviously, an S is a good grade, but the difference between that grade and those earned in the other courses allows for parents to compare against educational benchmarks. Further, very low grades in elementary school can help teachers and parents decide if a student needs to repeat a year in school to be better prepared for middle and high school.

Major Trends in High Schools

Unfortunately, there is a major trend for students in high school and college to receive more As. This is not occurring because the students are suddenly achieving at a higher level. Instead, it is the pressure of outside forces acting on school systems. You should strive to maintain your own belief of what constitutes A-quality work and not allow it to be compromised. Remember, if a student comes back a few years after leaving your class and he cannot read, people are going to question how he could possibly have received an A (or B or C) in your class.

Grading Too Low

Realize that if you give an inordinate amount of Ds or Fs, you will probably also receive a lot of questions from your administration. In fact, some administrations actively discourage giving low grades to students. It can be difficult as a new or inexperienced teacher to fight the administration on this particular issue. However, if you have a good reason to give low grades, and you have the evidence to prove that the student earned those grades, then you should definitely do it. Low scores should always be cause for reflection. An effective teacher should examine her methods and look for new ways to teach the material.

With that said, if you give a test or assignment that every student fails, you should take a deeper look at the reasons. As previously discussed, something may have been confusing or there may have been a problem with the wording, and you may want to consider throwing out the results. If the failures were caused by a lack of studying on your students' part, then definitely keep and use the scores.

QUESTION

Should the number of As you give equal the number of Fs?
Forcing grades to conform to a bell curve using arbitrary standards does more harm than good. It is better to teach effectively and assess validly, all the while working to help all students achieve A-level work.

Grading with Rubrics

Rubrics are an excellent way to grade assignments that are complicated or that would be difficult to grade objectively. Basically, a rubric lays out for the teacher what requirements each part of the assignment must meet to receive full or partial credit. When a teacher is grading an assignment like an essay, he can read through the assignment and compare this with the rubric to determine what grade to give. Rubrics are an excellent way to make your life easier while also letting students know exactly what is expected of them.

Creating Rubrics

The most time-consuming part of working with rubrics is creating effective ones. This should be done before you assign the students their work thereby providing you with a better understanding of exactly what you want your students to accomplish. You might even find that some of the assignment directions need to be changed in order to help the students do a better job.

Use the following to help guide your creation of rubrics:

1. List what you want your students to accomplish with the assignment.
2. Organize your list from most to least important.
3. Decide how much you want your assignment to be worth.
4. Assign each item from step 2 a percentage value with the total of all items equaling 100 percent.
5. Multiply your percentage value by the total value for the assignment to get the point value for each item.
6. Decide on specific grading criteria for each of the items.
7. Transfer this information into a chart with columns left blank for actual grade assigned and comments.
8. When you grade the assignment, use and attach this form.

As you can see, it is easier to grade if you know which categories you will be grading when you create your assignment.

FACT

Advanced Placement exams given by the College Board are graded using standard rubrics. Graders receive these rubrics and are trained in their use before they grade their first essay. This, along with other measures, assures consistency and fairness between graders.

Presenting Rubrics to Students

It is a good idea to present students with the rubric that you will use to grade their assignment when you first assign the work. This allows students to see exactly what you are going to be looking for as you grade. In fact, this is essential for elementary school students.

Some teachers find it useful to actually have students grade their own work based on the rubric before they turn in their assignment. This does not mean that you will use this grade, but it helps the students focus on the quality of their own work.

One final use of rubrics is for students to grade their peers. Unless you give the students a rubric from which to grade, they will not grade each other's work consistently.

Staying Organized

At times, keeping on top of grading can be a real challenge. For one thing, the short planning periods that teachers are given are usually not enough time to even begin grading all of the work that students turn in. In fact, elementary school teachers have very little planning time during the school day. This means that teachers spend a lot of their personal time grading work. Some teachers arrive at school early and some stay late. Others just take their work home with them. No matter when you choose to grade your students' work, grading takes time, so it is important that you find some strategies to lessen your grading time without cutting down on the quality of the grading or the work required of students.

Writing is an essential part of a quality education. Elementary school teachers must give numerous writing assignments to improve the students' skills. However, these writing assignments can often be difficult and time-consuming to grade. It is important that you devise grading methods to make your life easier.

ALERT

Colleges and businesses cite lack of writing skills as one of the major problems they face with new students and employees. It is important that teachers go beyond informal writing assignments and require their students to write formally.

First, you should create a rubric for each of your writing assignments. Your rubric should be consistent, with only the details changed in accordance with each topic. Your rubric should be convenient for you to use, so spend some time making your expectations very clear.

Grading by Comparison

One technique that may help you cut down on grading time is to read through the papers very quickly and place them in an order of quality across your desk or even on the floor. Then, when you are filling out the rubric, you will have some idea of what type of grade individual students should be earning, and you will be able to grade them in an order that makes sense for you. You might choose to grade either the best or worst work first. As you're using this method, you will find it easier to be consistent from paper to paper.

Large Assignments

If you give your students research papers or large projects to complete, it is imperative that you use rubrics to grade their work. Grading projects is often very subjective. Teachers will base some of the grade on the quality of the visuals or other artistic elements. Therefore, you need to make it very clear what is acceptable, or your students will not believe that you're being fair and consistent.

Daily Work

When you devise daily assignments, stay away from "busy work" if it does not truly reinforce or teach the students. Remember, you are going to have to grade whatever you assign. Therefore, if you are having students read through a section in the book and then answer questions, make sure the questions ask for information that you feel is important to learn.

Many teachers have students exchange papers and grade each other's work. This is definitely a time-saver. However, you need to make sure that you look through the students' grades each time to make sure no cheating occurred. You also need to check your school's policy on this, because some schools do not allow anyone except the teacher to grade student work.

Academic Integrity

You will be faced with integrity issues as you teach. The fact is that cheating is widespread, especially in later grades; students copy from each other or plagiarize work all the time. Some teachers choose to ignore this because the issue is difficult to deal with. However, if you truly want your students to be prepared, you must take a strong stand against cheating.

A Policy on Cheating

Most schools have discipline policies related to cheating and it is your responsibility to enforce this policy. It is not always easy to catch cheaters, however. While you might be able to catch someone looking at another student's paper during a test, it is much harder to catch someone who has an old copy of a test.

Therefore, it is a good idea for you to vary your tests from year to year. If you have a real problem, you can even vary them from class to class. If you are having an issue with students cheating during tests, surprise them with different forms of tests.

Sometimes catching cheaters seems like a losing proposition. Students are not easy to catch and are often very defensive when you do catch them. Parents sometimes have a hard time believing their children have cheated. However, if you believe in the integrity of the school system, then you have to keep trying.

FACT

A survey of 4,500 high school students, taken by the Rutgers Management Education Center, found that 75 percent of them seriously cheated. Further, many parents and students have very narrow definitions of what constitutes cheating. This is a huge problem that is causing great concern among educators.

It is important to realize that cheating will be a new concept to young students. In elementary grades, younger children might not understand the differences between collaboration and cheating. Therefore, it is important to provide examples of acceptable collaboration at a young age. If you help students understand these concepts early, it might help deter them from cheating in later grades.

Dealing with Plagiarism

Plagiarism is a specialized form of cheating in which students and others directly copy words or unique ideas from other sources. Sometimes students mistakenly plagiarize because they do not understand all the rules. They believe that as long as they cite their source they can copy something out of a book. It's important to teach your students exactly what plagiarism is before they begin working on any research projects.

It can often be difficult to catch students who have plagiarized. For one thing, it is often difficult to find the original source. This is where the Internet can help. Type a unique part of the suspected plagiarized work into a search engine to see if you come up with any exact matches. Special software to help teachers catch plagiarized text is also available.

However, if students have used printed materials not available online or are not listed on search engines, then you will have a hard time finding the source. When this occurs, you will have to rely on methods such as comparing the writing structure of the student's normal work to that of the suspected passage. If there are big words in the passage, you could ask the student to define the words for you. You could even ask him to explain what he has written in his own words.

It's Not Easy to Catch

None of this is an exact science. It is a sad fact that students can go online and buy research papers. Technically, this isn't plagiarism, and it's hard to catch. Your best defense for catching plagiarism and cheating might be a good offense. Consider requiring an oral defense of all research papers to be presented in front of the class. Even if students buy their papers, they will still have to master the material in order to answer your questions.

CHAPTER 13

High-Stakes Testing

Assessments are an integral part of all students' educational careers. Most classroom tests are simply one part of the overall curriculum, and the score on any one test usually does not mean the difference between success and failure in the course. This is not the case with high-stakes testing. As the name implies, this type of test has huge consequences for the test taker and often for the teacher and the school.

What Is High-Stakes Testing?

High-stakes testing is a practice in which the outcome on a standardized test is used as a determining factor in decisions concerning students. Examples of consequences for students include being held back in a grade or not being allowed to graduate until the test is passed. High-stakes testing has a long history and it is still widely used in the United States today.

FACT

Approximately 80 percent of U.S. government jobs today are filled using work experience, background, and education as qualifications. Only the remaining 20 percent require applicants to pass a written test. Examples of these jobs include air traffic controllers and law enforcement personnel.

Examples of High-Stakes Testing

According to *The Big Test: The Secret History of the American Meritocracy,* by Nicholas Lemann, James Bryant Conant initially developed the Standardized Achievement Test (SAT) to help eliminate the predominance of individuals who were rewarded because of their personal connections or their wealth. It's still thought that the SAT provides a merit-based method for comparison among students. The American College Testing (ACT) assessment was created in 1959 to compete with the SAT. Today, many students take both tests, and each college has its own preference for which score(s) to use for admission purposes.

However, some people have questioned whether these standardized tests have achieved their goals. Results have created a huge conflict over race and test bias. The reasons for this are varied and beyond the scope of this book. Suffice it to say, however, that this issue has implications on the future of standardized testing and on your job as an educator.

Determining college acceptance criteria is not the only use of high-stakes exams. Many states also use high-stakes testing for determination of course mastery and decisions concerning promotion and graduation. The following is just a short sample list of state tests at this time:

- **California:** Students must pass the California High School Exit Examination in order to graduate.
- **Florida:** Students from grades three to ten take various forms of the Florida Comprehensive Assessment Test (FCAT), and results have consequences for the school and for graduation eligibility.
- **New York:** Students take Regents Exams, some of which must be passed for graduation and some of which make a student eligible for an Advanced Regents Diploma.
- **Texas:** Students from grades four to eleven take various forms of the Texas Assessment of Knowledge and Skills; students must pass the eleventh grade test to graduate.

As this sampling shows, failing high-stakes state tests can have a huge impact on students. All fifty states have standardized tests of one sort or another that they use to judge their educational system.

Current Trends

According to the *No Child Left Behind Act of 2001*, states are required to administer academic assessments of students in grades four and eight for reading and math. States may also choose to conduct assessments of reading and math in grade twelve. This reinforces the trend of more states instituting standardized tests, many of which at least partially determine funding for schools and graduation eligibility.

Proponents of this act claim that increased standardized testing will lead to greater teacher accountability concerning student learning. Further, it is believed that if students are at least proficient enough to pass the exams, then they have received a basic, sound education. Opponents of the plan, on the other hand, feel that it is inappropriate to put so much weight on one exam. They often feel that test bias or test anxiety can adversely affect scores and therefore render the tests inaccurate.

While politicians and educational leaders continue arguing over this issue, day-to-day teachers have little control over what happens. As a teacher, your only option is to make the best of the decisions that are handed down to you.

What's at Stake

As already indicated, many state exams have consequences for students, teachers, and schools. Student promotion and graduation are often tied to these exams. Further, many states now base at least a portion of school funding on student test performance.

Effect on Students

Standardized testing in and of itself is not a bad idea. It is definitely better to reward someone for their merit as opposed to their personal connections. However, high-stakes testing can have unforeseen consequences for students, especially at elementary levels. For one thing, high-stakes standardized testing must be based on the body of knowledge students actually learn in order to be valid. Unfortunately, even the best tests require that students spend extra time on test preparation—which means less time spent on learning. In the elementary grades, where many students are still learning foundational knowledge that they will need through the rest of their school years, time spent on preparing for tests that do not mirror the curriculum is time wasted.

QUESTION

How do you determine if a test is biased?
If, on average, groups of the same ability level (as judged by other methods) earn scores that are statistically different from their peers, the test may be considered biased. For example, if men and women of the same ability have different average scores, the test may be biased.

Beyond the fact that students might be missing important instruction to prepare for high-stakes tests, students from lower socioeconomic backgrounds often score lower on standardized tests. This could be because of the level of education they are receiving, the amount of time they spend practicing, or even test bias. The belief among opponents of high-stakes testing is that the pressure of these types of tests can be harmful to these and other disadvantaged students.

According to a study by the National Board on Educational Testing and Public Policy (NBETPP), two of the negative effects of standardized tests on students include test-related stress and unfairness to special populations. On the flip side, some individuals in the poll cited an increase in student motivation and an overall increase in the quality of education.

The effects of testing on students are hard to measure because students have their own individual attitudes toward tests. Obviously, students with test anxiety or other test-taking difficulties will have the hardest time with these types of assessments.

Effect on Schools

In many states, schools are also heavily affected by the results of standardized testing. For example, in Florida, elementary, middle, and high schools are given a grade on a scale from A to F. The school's grade is based on many standards, including how its students achieved and improved on the FCAT. Schools that achieve high grades earn financial rewards.

Additionally, when a school first earns an F, it gets increased state aid. However, if the school continues to receive low grades, the state may intervene. One of the effects of this intervention is to provide students with vouchers called Opportunity Scholarships. Through this program, affected students can choose to attend higher-performing public schools.

Obviously, the stakes in this type of atmosphere make high achievement on the FCAT a top priority. Many elementary schools have instituted required FCAT practice times in all classes, closed campuses during testing weeks, and provided pizza parties or other rewards once the testing is complete. Students are given lectures by their teachers on the importance of tests. And free breakfast is provided in many schools to ensure that hunger will not affect test results.

Arguments for High-Stakes Testing

There are many people who believe that high-stakes standardized testing is a necessary element of the educational system. Only with real rewards and consequences will students and schools rise in their level of achievement. In fact, student motivation is one of the arguments for high-stakes testing.

Because these tests are required for promotion and/or graduation, students have a real motivating factor for achievement. Other reasons people argue for the use of high-stakes testing include holding educators accountable and providing measures of comparison.

ESSENTIAL

Different national groups have differing opinions on high-stakes testing. The American Federation of Teachers (AFT) supports the use of exit exams. The National Education Association (NEA), on the other hand, believes important issues like graduation should not depend on one standardized test.

Holding Educators Accountable

Many people believe that in the United States today, the state of education is a mess, and unfortunately, they think that teachers are mostly to blame. The fact is that because of low pay, the effects of tenure, and the loosening of certification requirements, some teachers are just not very good. Proponents believe that standardized high-stakes testing forces teachers to cover at least a minimum of quality information for students.

Proponents also feel that high-stakes testing provides a measure of accountability where very few other measures exist. Grading practices differ from teacher to teacher and are therefore not valid for comparison and accountability. On the other hand, state tests are valid because all students are measured using the same test. Students either are or are not prepared for these exams based on the education they have received from their teachers.

Providing Measures for Comparison

How can you compare one school to another? Without standard measures, parents rely on word of mouth and rumor. Schools are labeled as good or bad based on parent and student perceptions of the quality of their education. Proponents of high-stakes testing claim that these tests allow the public a means for comparing schools.

Since lower-income schools are also often the poorest performing, this means of measure has huge implications in terms of educational responsibility. High-stakes testing proponents claim that by exposing disparities, more assistance can be given to these schools and, more importantly, their students. This support has come in various ways, including increased scrutiny and even aid from state agencies.

Arguments Against High-Stakes Testing

Even as proponents cite important benefits for the implementation of high-stakes testing, opponents claim that there are reasons to support its elimination. They argue that these tests do not mirror curriculum, that they put students under undue pressure, and that they are often perceived as being biased against minority students and students from lower socioeconomic backgrounds.

ESSENTIAL

High-stakes testing often puts a lot of pressure on you as a teacher. However, you need to avoid letting any stress you feel from this pressure affect your day-to-day teaching.

Tests Do Not Mirror Curriculum

Many people argue that the standardized tests do not test what students are actually learning in their courses. Therefore, teachers have to stop teaching their required curriculum in order to spend time helping students pass the tests. If the tests are properly constructed, this is not the case. However, opponents argue that many times the tests are not well constructed. They test "artificial" information that does not truly show student achievement.

Undue Pressure

Opponents also argue that high-stakes testing puts too much pressure on students and teachers. They claim that students can actually be harmed by the amount of emphasis placed on passing these exams. Because there is so much discussion and pressure put on the students, it is not uncommon for them to really worry about passing these tests. It is sad when a group of advanced third graders who should have little, if any, problem in passing the third grade standardized exam are so worried about passing that they feel sick going into the test. However, this happens all the time. There is a question of whether test anxieties can actually result in invalid grades.

Standardized Testing Is Biased

People who believe that high-stakes testing is a bad practice also cite the bias that appears to be inherent in standardized testing. Minority students and those from lower-income families get lower scores, on average, on these tests. Therefore, using them as a method for comparison between schools is not valid and is actually harmful.

The Impact on You

You will be affected by standardized testing in one way or another. If you are not teaching in a year when a high-stakes test is given, you will in many instances be required to provide students with advance instruction on the types of questions they will face in the coming years. If you are teaching in grades where these high-stakes tests are taken, you will probably be required to spend at least some time directly preparing students for their exam. If a lot of students fail these exams, questions will be asked of their school and their teachers. People will want to know why they were not better prepared.

However, teachers are under the greatest pressure when funding is tied to results of standardized tests. In these instances, teachers in all grades are pushed to spend time preparing students for their exams. If the tests mirror the curriculum students are to learn anyway, this is not a major burden. However, if the opposite is true, then teachers might find they spend more time preparing students for the tests than teaching required material. However, it is important not to spend time complaining to the students about the worthiness of the exams. This could have an adverse affect because students might not take the tests seriously.

Teaching to the Test

Is teaching to the test a bad thing? The answer depends on the test in question. If it's a well-constructed test that actually measures what a student should have learned, teaching to the test is a good idea. You would be teaching what the students should already be learning through the curriculum. Aside from a few days of specific preparation for the test questions, teachers would not have to make major changes to their lessons.

ALERT

Today, high-stakes tests are being used more and more often to evaluate teacher performance. It's a good idea to work with the other teachers at your school to come up with a plan for improving test scores among your students. If your school is deemed to be underperforming, this could have personal consequences for you.

On the other hand, if the test in question is poorly constructed, and it does not measure what students should have learned, then teaching to the test means that educators are not teaching students what they need to know. Instead of following the state and national standards, teachers might only include information relevant to the test. This is especially true when the stakes involved are high. Therefore, these students might become excellent at taking a particular test, but they will fail to understand what they should really be learning.

Testing is not inherently bad. However, students must be tested on the information that they should have learned in the first place. Only when this occurs will "teaching the curriculum" and "teaching to the test" mean the same thing.

CHAPTER 14

Beyond the Classroom

During your teaching career, you will take students on trips outside of the traditional classroom. You may go on field trips, actually leaving campus and visiting an outside location. Or these may be virtual field trips, in which students visit a computer lab and take a trip around the Internet. These trips might be as close to home as going to the media center. Leaving the classroom can present new learning opportunities—and new problems.

Are Field Trips Worth It?

Some people question the necessity of field trips and whether the headaches are worth the benefits. However, sometimes a trip outside the school environment can reinforce important concepts or ideas better than time in the classroom can. For a field trip to be a success, though, you have to take the time to thoroughly prepare your students for the experience.

On the Bright Side

There are many reasons to take students on field trips:

- They provide the students with a different method of learning.
- They often broaden the students' horizons and expose them to new and different topics.
- They reinforce concepts learned in the classroom.
- They provide shared reference points that can be used in later lessons.
- They help you see your students in a different light while allowing them to see a different side of you too.

On field trips, students learn by doing something instead of just sitting passively. If you take students to a hands-on museum, they will have a lot of fun and they will learn at the same time. Further, exposing students to new information helps expand their point of view. This added exposure could be especially rewarding for students from a lower socioeconomic background, who may not have these experiences otherwise.

If you cover difficult or challenging material in class, seeing it presented in a new way can really help reinforce the information. For example, learning about sound waves is a lot different than going to a museum and actually experiencing them in different mediums. Further, you can provide yourself with reference points for the rest of the school year. You can refer to different things the students saw or experienced and use them as you teach.

Probably the most overlooked positive aspect of going on field trips is the opportunity to see your students in a different light. Often very quiet students will open up in these kinds of situations. Further, your students will also see you in a new way because you are not standing in front of the classroom. They will observe how you interact with them in a less formal manner and also how you handle situations that might arise. Do not underestimate the importance of being a good role model at all times, even if the bus driver does take a wrong turn.

ESSENTIAL

Make sure that students realize exactly what you expect from them in terms of behavior. Consequences for major misbehaviors should be severe. Many teachers bar students who misbehave from ever participating in any future field trips.

On the Other Hand

There are also negative aspects associated with taking students on field trips. The following list presents a few of them:

- It will require more planning time.
- You have to deal with some red tape.
- You have to collect money and get chaperones.
- You have to keep your students organized.
- Students have more freedom, which may lead to discipline issues.
- Your destination might not turn out to be what you expected.

It takes a lot of time to effectively plan a field trip. You must coordinate arrangements and transportation. You have to fill out paperwork and get permission. You have to collect permission slips and money. You have to get chaperones and create your student groups. All of these tasks can lead to a monumental headache for you. If you do not follow through on each of these issues, then you will probably have a bad time on your field trip.

Further, students have more freedom on field trips. Often, you will be separated with your own small group and will not know what is going on in the other groups. Therefore, you will not be able to control your students as you would in the classroom. It is very important that you set up strict rules beforehand and inform the students of heavy consequences for misbehavior. Remember that the way your students behave reflects on you and your school. It is not unheard of for destinations to forbid certain schools from ever visiting again because of major misbehaviors.

Finally, your field trip might not turn out the way you expected. For example, you might get to your destination to find that the descriptions do not live up to reality. What you thought would be fun and interesting for your students might turn out to be boring. You might also find that your class takes a lot less time to complete their activities. Therefore, you have to wait some time before the buses are scheduled to pick you up. It is always wise to plan for such occurrences before you leave.

ALERT

Keep track of your students at all times. Do frequent head counts and require that your chaperones do the same. Also, select a central meeting place that is easily identifiable and tell your students that if they do get separated from the group, they are to return to that location and wait there.

Field Trip Destinations

Your choices of destinations for field trips will depend on where you live and what your school will allow. Some examples of common field trips include the following:

- Hands-on museums
- Traditional museums
- Historical and archaeological sites
- Zoos
- Nature trails
- Theme parks

Whatever your destination, you need to make sure that you have thoroughly researched it before going. It is best to actually visit the location before taking your students there. At the very least, you should get a detailed map and information concerning exactly what will be scheduled for the students during the day.

Some destinations require teachers to schedule their field trips a great deal of time in advance. For example, the Smithsonian National Museum of American History requires that any visits be scheduled a minimum of four weeks in advance. Popular locations will fill up early, so check with your destination.

Theme-park trips are a special case because students are usually under the least control at these places. If you want the students to have an educational experience and not just ride the latest roller coaster, make sure to have a purpose for your trip. For example, you might be participating in a physics day, where students have to fill out worksheets concerning the laws of physics as they apply to roller coasters and other rides. Going to a theme park just for the fun of it needs serious consideration. If it is a "reward" for some huge deed, then it might be acceptable, though it still needs to be approved by the administration.

Planning the Field Trip

Field trips require a lot of planning and preparation on your part. You need to consider all the implications and concerns about taking your class outside of the school. If you feel that you can handle a field trip, the first thing you need to do is check your school's policies concerning field trips.

Preliminary Plans

Before you make any reservations for a field trip, you must consult your administration and get your trip approved. Many times, you will be required to fill out a proposal that includes purpose, date, and destination. Once you have received your approval, you will immediately want to make your reservations for your destination and your transportation.

Make sure to check with your school about the policy concerning transportation for students. Some schools allow you to use traditional school buses, which are usually cheaper. Others require use of specific commercial bus lines.

One final thing you might want to consider deals with lunches. If you are taking students somewhere where they will be required to buy their lunch, you might have students who are on free or reduced lunches that need to be taken into consideration. Many districts have policies that you must provide these students with lunches while they are on their field trip. Therefore, you should make advance arrangements with your lunchroom to create "bag lunches" for these students.

Should participation in a field trip be required for all students?
Many schools have determined that you cannot force students to participate in field trips. Therefore, you will probably also need to schedule for a substitute during the day of your field trip for students who are left behind. Make sure that you create a lesson for those students while you are gone.

Collecting Money

Once you have made your reservations, you determine the cost for each student to participate. Students should be required to turn in their permission slips and money at the same time. It is important that you set up a system for helping students who cannot afford to go on the field trip. Talk with your school and fellow teachers about ways that you can get a little money to help these students.

As you're collecting cash, make sure that you do not mix it with your own money. There are legal issues involved with the collection of money, so it is very important that you keep a careful accounting of what you have collected.

Chaperones and Student Groups

You will probably need to get volunteers to help chaperone your field trip. Most schools have guidelines setting the maximum number of students of each age group that you should have per chaperone. Use the guidelines and your common sense to guide you. Remember, parents and other volunteers often do not have the same handle on discipline as you do because they do not have the day-to-day experience with your students.

It is a good idea to mention any upcoming field trips to parents whenever you call them or at parent conferences. This allows you the opportunity to directly ask them to volunteer. You should also send home a detailed announcement of any upcoming field trip with a call for volunteers.

Most destinations will also have rules concerning student-to-chaperone ratios. For example, the Chicago Museum of Science and Industry requires one chaperone for every five students aged six and under and one for every ten students over six.

Once you have the required number of chaperones, you will want to create your groups. Make sure that you take some time to truly consider whom you are putting together in a group. If you have two students who traditionally are fine when they are by themselves but together cause a lot of mischief, you should consider separating them on the field trip. Similarly, if you have two students who just cannot get along, it is best to separate them into different groups. Try not to place more than one really challenging student in each group. That way it will be easier to control each group. Be nice to your volunteers so that they will continue to help out in the future.

QUESTION

What do I do if a student doesn't have either lunch or lunch money?
Never let a student go hungry. If a student doesn't have lunch, you will need to let him borrow money to buy it. If this becomes a frequent problem, you might ask your administration for a small discretionary fund to be used during field trips.

One question that often arises is whether to place a student with his or her parent. Generally, this is a good idea. However, some students do misbehave more when they are with their own parents. If you have concerns about this, you might want to discuss it with the parent and student before creating your groups.

Finally, try to balance your groups by gender. In other words, do not place all boys or all girls in a group. This is mainly done for the chaperone. As experience teaches us, boys in earlier grades tend to be more rambunctious than girls.

You also might consider having all chaperones and teachers wear a distinctive color. For example, you could all wear red or yellow. This will help students spot you when you are at your destination.

Creating the Lesson

It's important to prepare the students for the field trip. You need to make it clear that they are going to have fun, but they are also going to learn. For that purpose, you should prepare learning activities for them to complete during the field trip.

For example, you can create worksheets for the students to fill out as they're learning new information. A treasure or scavenger hunt is another good idea. Have students look for specific items and answer questions about them as they go through the museum. Some destinations even provide teachers with this type of material. The places you visit will more than likely be willing to help you create an effective lesson because it makes their job easier, too.

ESSENTIAL

You should attempt to minimize complaints about field trip groupings by posting the groups close to the time of your field trip. Make very strict rules concerning changes in group composition. Once you move one student, others will ask for this privilege too.

Contingency Plans

Take some time to consider what your students will do if things do not work out as planned. For example, what would happen if the field trip took a lot less time than expected? Try to find out if there is anything else you can do to fill up time. Some museums are located in or near parks, so this might be an alternative for your students.

Field Trip Day

On field trip days, you will want to arrive at school early to complete last-minute preparations. While waiting for buses to arrive, you need to take attendance and organize the groups. (Make sure that you are aware of all school policies concerning permission slips and attendance before you leave.) If you have planned all the details of your field trip, then you should have an effective and enjoyable day.

The day after your field trip, you should definitely take some time to discuss the experience with your students. Reinforce what you wanted them to learn from the trip. Allow them to give you their impressions so that you can decide whether to visit that destination again with other classes. You might even consider having an assignment on what they learned during the field trip.

ALERT

Any time you leave on a field trip, make sure you know the location of first-aid supplies on your bus and at your destination. If an accident occurs, you will be able to take charge of the situation quickly and effectively.

Virtual Field Trips

Field trips no longer have to take place off campus, but can now occur at any Internet-connected computer. Many sites have created excellent Internet field trips for your students to complete. You can also create such a field trip by going to a website and creating your own information scavenger hunt. For example, you might go to the NASA website and create questions based on the information offered there.

Pros and Cons

Obviously, a lot less planning is required for this type of field trip—all you have to do is reserve the computers and create your lesson plan. Plus, you can "take" students to places they may never visit, like the Louvre or Colonial Williamsburg. You can show them the wealth of resources that are available to them through the Internet.

On the other hand, virtual field trips are less interactive than actual field trips. Some students might have a hard time getting into the field trip on a computer. Further, if you have slow Internet access, your field trip might take an inordinate amount of time. Finally, lessons you create have to be updated frequently as websites often go up, shut down, or get changed significantly. The URLs that worked yesterday may no longer be active today.

Visits to the Media Center

Most teachers take their students to the media center at one time or another. Just as with field trips, it is important that you plan exactly what you want students to do while they are there. Further, it is very important that students know and follow the rules that you establish. Check with your media center to find out how to reserve time for your students. Many schools only allow a limited number of classes in each period and these time slots will often fill up quickly. If you are planning on having students write a research paper, then you will want to block out the required time as soon as you can.

Making Visits Productive

When you take your class to the media center, your students must have a clear purpose for being there. For example, if you are working on research papers in class, it is important to give students time to research at the library. However, if you simply let them go to the media center each day without requiring daily progress reports, you may find they have wasted their time.

Make goals for students each day you are in the media center. For example, if your class is working on research papers, a student's goal for one day might be to find and report on three or more possible sources. You can judge whether you have given them enough work if many students complete the minimum requirements and then try to turn to other work or spend time doing personal things. It is imperative that you circulate among your students to make sure they are on task.

Importance of Rules

It is very important that students behave while they are in the media center. Rightly or wrongly, their behavior is a reflection on you. Media center personnel will often bend over backward to help teachers. However, teachers who have horrible discipline skills will not get the same consideration. (The importance of staying on friendly terms with media center personnel and other staff is discussed in greater depth in Chapter 18.)

CHAPTER 15

Avoiding Stress and Illness

Much is expected of you as a teacher. With the daily demands on your time, it is no wonder that health concerns often fall by the wayside and stress is a rampant problem among teachers. However, you cannot be an effective teacher if you aren't in good health—or if you aren't a happy and satisfied person. It's important that you take steps to combat illness and stress in order to make your life better and to be a great teacher.

Expect to Get Sick

Each year, teachers are exposed to many new germs. Every time a paper is handed in or a student borrows one of your pencils, you will be exposed to germs. If you have a shared computer, then you are also subject to further exposure. In fact, you may come in contact with germs you're not resistant to just by touching the handle to open your door.

New teachers are especially vulnerable. In most cases, the new teacher's body is simply not immune to all of the germs it will encounter. As a new teacher, you should expect to take all of the sick days you have available to you. However, there are some steps you can take to keep yourself and your students healthier.

Practice Prevention

Make sure that you wash your hands often and use antibacterial hand wash during class. Have this type of hand sanitizer available for student use. If students in your class are sneezing or coughing a lot, make sure that when they leave the classroom you clean their desks and the door handle along with anything else they might have touched. You should also make sure to take a daily multivitamin and to drink plenty of fluids. Healthy eating habits lead to better overall health.

If it is the cold and flu season and all your students seem to be catching the latest bug, you might consider avoiding assignments that require them to work in close groups. When students work in groups, they often share pens, pencils, and papers. They also usually sit closer together than normal, thus leading to a greater chance of exposure and illness.

Teaching Students to Be Thoughtful

Many teachers catch the latest bugs from students. For example, students will come up to your desk and sneeze or cough in your face without covering their mouths. While it is understandable that a kindergartner or first-grader might do this, it just seems inexcusable in a senior. However, this is the situation you may experience as a teacher in any grade.

Even though you are not your students' parent or guardian, you should still take some time to teach them important life skills and manners. Just as you would remind her to say "please" and "thank you," you should also point out whenever a student does not cover her mouth when sneezing and tell her it is not acceptable. Continuing to reinforce manners will make a difference in the long run.

FACT

Each year more than 200,000 people in the United States are hospitalized and approximately 36,000 people die because of the flu. January and February are typically the worst months for the flu, even though the flu season can last from November through March.

Be Your Own Best Sub

There is nothing shameful about staying home when you are really sick. However, there will be times when you are definitely not at your best but still not sick enough to stay home and use a sick day. These are the days when you need to learn to be your own best sub.

Being your own best sub means that you are not going to put a ton of energy into your lesson for the day. You might have the students copy notes, watch a pertinent and educationally sound movie, or give the students worksheets to complete in class. Of course this is not the way you should typically run your classroom. However, it is perfectly acceptable to do this every once in a while. Even on days when you are "subbing" for yourself, students will achieve more educationally than on days when actual subs are running your class.

Getting Hurt on the Job

Getting hurt on the job is a daily occurrence in schools across the nation. It is important to know your rights and if you get hurt, to take full advantage of the worker's compensation laws. You need to protect yourself, so make sure that you fully understand the procedures and that you follow through.

Reporting Injuries

The first thing you must do in order to qualify for worker's compensation is to report your injury to your school. You will probably have to fill out an accident report describing exactly what happened. You should do this even if you think your injury is minor or you are not planning to visit a doctor. This will protect and cover you if something related to your injury arises once you get home or over the next few days. Sometimes injuries that seem minor worsen over time. Just make sure to cover all bases, and fill out any necessary paperwork when an injury does occur.

Getting Medical Attention

If you are hurt, usually your school will send you to a doctor that handles the district's worker's compensation cases. Make sure to see this doctor if you have any questions at all about the extent of your injury. Read up on your rights concerning second opinions and understand exactly what you should expect from the school if you require extensive medical attention or time away from the classroom.

ESSENTIAL

According to the Occupational Safety and Health Administration (OSHA), in 2001, there were 3.4 nonfatal injuries per 100 full-time workers in elementary and secondary schools. Of those individual injuries, one-third resulted in lost time at work.

Do not wait to get medical attention, even if you do not think you are that severely injured. Small problems can easily lead to more complications if not taken care of properly.

Sick Buildings

The hazards of teaching are not limited to work-related injuries. Unfortunately, just being present at some schools can cause health problems. This is because some school buildings are actually "sick" themselves. This does not mean that the building has a cold. Instead, it means that for one reason or another, dangerous pathogens are afloat in the air and can cause sickness through inhalation.

Likely Causes

Most of the time, a poor ventilation system is to blame for the problem. If the air conditioning unit in your school building is too small, this can lead to many problems. Buildings that were built to be airtight and don't have opening windows can also have similar ventilation problems.

As dust builds up in ducts throughout the building, pathogens, mold spores, and other illness-causing molecules thrive. When this infectious dust begins circulating through the ventilation system, it becomes airborne and can cause people to become sick. Lack of air filters and other clean-air equipment means these particles collect inside the school.

FACT

According to the Environmental Protection Agency (EPA), poor indoor air quality can lead to greater student absences. It has also been associated with poor student performance in areas like concentration, memory, and calculation.

Common Symptoms

How do you know if you are working in a sick building? There are many symptoms to watch for; if you see yourself or many of your fellow teachers experiencing the following, you should probably take some action.

- Frequent headaches
- Itchy, watery eyes
- Chronic fatigue
- Dizziness
- Problems with pregnancy and miscarriage
- Cough or sore throat
- Skin problems
- Nausea
- Cancer

Feeling better when you spend time away from the school building is another good indicator to watch for. Do the symptoms disappear over long breaks? If so, then they might be related to the building.

Take Action

If you experience any of the above symptoms routinely, and you feel it is related to the building where you work, this should be reported. And you should also notify your administration of any mold growths you notice in the school building. Unfortunately, it can be difficult for new teachers to take action. You may not be on a permanent contract and protected by tenure, and you may not want to make waves. It's also possible that you've heard horror stories about other teachers who reported problems and were subsequently transferred or fired.

However, your health should be your first concern. Record your symptoms over a period of time. If you notice mold growing, make sure that you take pictures of it because they might be important in future proceedings. You can try to speak tactfully with your direct supervisor to see if anything happens. However, sometimes you might just have to go directly to the OSHA and the EPA in order to have them test the air quality. If you do this, others must join in your complaint.

ESSENTIAL

Keep a diary of your illnesses if you believe they are related to the indoor air quality at school. This will be useful when you go to your school administrator or other officials to lodge a complaint.

If you can prove that you have been injured by the quality of the air, you are eligible to receive workman's compensation. Your school will also be required to make special accommodations for you under the *Americans with Disabilities Act (ADA)*. You may even be given early retirement under certain circumstances. However, realize that it is often difficult to get a doctor to agree that the cause of your illness was definitely the building where you work.

Causes of Stress

There are many causes of stress in a teacher's life—administrative red tape, student disruptions, noise, the demands of the job, and the personal pressure teachers put on themselves each day. If you often feel your heart pounding and are always on edge, then you are experiencing stress. Over time, this wears on your body and can cause you to be very sick. The effects of stress can lead to illness and even death, so it is not something to play around with. Before you learn how to manage your stress, you need to figure out what causes it.

External Factors

Most of the stress you will experience as a teacher will be caused by your job. External forces will be pulling you in many different directions. Some of the biggest stress for teachers comes with major changes in their school. It seems that at some schools the administration feels the need to make significant changes each summer. These changes might range from switching to a different class schedule to changing the entire structure of the school.

ALERT

Stress is related to digestive problems, such as constipation and ulcers. It is also connected with headaches and migraines. People who have very stressful jobs are more prone to heart attacks and high blood pressure.

Another huge source of stress comes from the students themselves. Most students you will encounter are courteous and respectful. However, every year there will be at least one class that you dread. Often, the reason is one or a few students who give you grief—and if you do not have a good handle on discipline, the misbehaviors that arise will be very hard to take. Another source of stress comes from noise. If you cannot keep your students quiet and under control, you could be headed for disaster.

Internal Factors

Teachers are often toughest on themselves; they expect a lot of themselves each and every day. If you never allow yourself to make a mistake or have an off day, you will eventually burn out. You must find a way to stay grounded as you go through the school year. Remember what is really important to you as you approach each day. The fact is that internal stressors are often the hardest to change.

Stress Relief

Stress relief begins and ends with your mind. You need to realize that you do not and cannot have control over every situation. Sometimes the administration will make choices that entirely change your work life. Unfortunately, you will not have any say in the matter. Students will misbehave in class, and even though you are in charge, you cannot always control these situations before they arise. The only thing that you can have complete control over is your own feelings and perceptions.

When stressful situations arise, choose to act and not react. Instead of sitting back and wallowing in misery, jump in and try to find ways to solve any problems or issues that arise. Even if you do not get your way in the end, just the act of getting involved will help you feel better.

ESSENTIAL

Take some time to do something for yourself each day. Take a nice stroll in the evening or read a good book. Even a little bit of quiet time to unwind can be a huge help toward reducing your stress.

Stress-Relieving Habits

Getting enough sleep, exercising, and practicing good eating habits are extremely important in fighting stress. Relaxation is the key to lower stress levels. When you feel that you're in a stressful situation, remember to breathe deeply. As you breathe in, scrunch up your entire body and then let it out at once, and you will begin to relax.

Remember not to sweat the small stuff. While this may be an old cliché, it is still valid. When a stressful situation arises, consider if you will even remember it tomorrow or next week. The fact is that most situations are momentary. Getting stressed about them leads to nothing but illness.

Sleep Deprivation

If you have ever been around a tired, cranky child, you know that sleep deprivation can seriously affect your mood and your attitude. Lack of sleep is a major cause of illness and stress for teachers and students alike. Sleep problems can lead to more mistakes and difficulty in concentrating. Make sure that you understand the symptoms of sleep deprivation, and take the time to get a good night's sleep each night.

People who are sleep deprived are often grumpy and cannot seem to keep their eyes open. Many times they are unable to concentrate for long periods of time. Their stress levels are usually higher than normal and their personalities might change. They might also experience memory loss.

Dealing with Sleep Deprivation

You should try to keep regular hours and go to bed at the same time each night. If you constantly vary your bedtime, you will end up confusing your body, which can lead to further sleep problems. Avoid caffeine and refrain from exercise just before going to bed. Try to relax. Some people find that if their minds are racing, they can get some rest if they take the time to write down everything they are thinking about.

Another strategy to consider is creating your own "going to sleep" routine. Children do a better job going to sleep each night when they have a bedtime routine. You should follow this example and always do the same things as you prepare to sleep.

Finally, if you just cannot get to sleep, it is best to get up and do something restful. Some people find that if they read, this will help them fall asleep more quickly. However, make sure that whatever you do, you do not turn on bright lights. If you follow these steps, you should be well on your way to being a more rested and healthy person.

CHAPTER 16

Giving Substitutes a Fighting Chance

Substitutes have a very difficult job. They come into a classroom that they probably never visited before, and must control a class of thirty or more students while trying to follow the lesson plan the teacher left behind. As everyone knows, students are prone to giving substitutes a very hard time. Even the best students will often misbehave when a substitute is in charge. Your best chance to alleviate a possibly volatile situation is to fully prepare your substitute and your students.

The Substitute Folder

Substitutes need direction when they come into your class. They need to know your seating chart and your discipline plan. They also need to know what you wish for them to cover during the class period. Most problems occur for substitutes when they are not given the information they need to be effective. One way that you can provide the necessary information to your substitutes is to create a substitute folder.

For a Purpose

The substitute folder is the point of reference for all substitutes who come to your room. This folder should always be kept in the same spot on your desk. Some teachers will actually pull their substitute folder out and place it on the center of their desk each evening just in case an emergency arises and they miss the next day.

ALERT

Do not leave personal documents or belongings on or in unlocked parts of your desk. It is not necessarily the substitute you need to be concerned about. Substitutes often have problems controlling student behavior. You do not want students having access to your personal information when the substitute is otherwise occupied.

A substitute folder provides substitutes with all of the information they need to feel confident in your classroom. It informs them of your policies and procedures, and it allows them to communicate with you about the events of the day by leaving you notes and other papers in the substitute folder.

The Folder's Contents

Your substitute folder should be distinctive in color and have the words "Substitute Folder" written in large letters. What you choose to include in the folder is up to you. At a bare minimum, consider adding the following:

- Substitute information form
- Seating chart

- Discipline referrals
- Attendance sheets
- Daily class schedule
- Specific student information
- Hall passes
- Additional helpful notes
- Extra paper for the substitute teacher's comments to you

The substitute information form should include important information about your class, the school, and the teachers who teach in nearby classes. An example of this type of form is included in the CD that comes with this book. Your daily class schedule is especially important if your school runs on a modified or block schedule. Without this guidance, substitute teachers may not know when classes begin and end or when they should take lunch.

Specific student information refers to notes that might be helpful to a substitute while they are teaching. For example, if you have a student who has a special medical privilege to use the restroom, you should include this as a note. Further, if you have two students who do not get along very well, you might want to let the substitute know, so she can keep them separated.

You should also leave some extra blank paper for notes. Substitutes can write down their concerns and other information for you. It can then be placed inside the substitute folder, and you can refer to it when you return.

ESSENTIAL

It is important to let substitutes know specific information to help them deal with special situations in your classroom. However, you must always keep the students' privacy in mind. Therefore, make sure that you are not sharing sensitive information that is unnecessary for the substitute to know in order to do an effective job.

If you know that you will be absent, leave a lesson plan in the substitute folder. It is also a good idea to write the day's agenda on the board. This will give the substitute and students something to refer to during the class. It will also help cut down on confusion between the students and the substitute. Remember, a well-informed substitute is an effective substitute.

Effective Substitute Lesson Plans

If you want something productive to happen in your classroom when a substitute is present, you must leave a lesson plan. Just as you use a lesson plan to guide what you do each day, substitutes will turn to your lesson plan for guidance. The plan also gives them something to rely on when students question them about the validity of the work. The substitute can simply say, "This is what your teacher left, so you'll have to talk to him about it tomorrow."

What to Include

In the same way you create your own lesson plans, you must determine what you want students to learn while you are gone and how much they should finish in one class period. Generally, you should realize that students will not give substitute lessons as much credence as your own lessons. However, this should not keep you from having two or three important points that they should take away from the substitute's lesson. You can write these on the board before you leave or have the substitute write them at the beginning of class to reinforce their importance.

Do not try something new or complicated with a substitute. For example, do not try a simulation or role-play—these activities can easily get out of hand. The freedom inherent in these types of activities can often lead to disruptions that can be hard for a substitute to manage. You want to minimize activities that can lead to problems.

Typically, you should leave assignments that require students to copy some notes you have left behind or read quietly from their textbooks. Then ask them to answer some questions or complete some other type of written assignment. You could also ask them to take a short quiz on the information.

How Much to Include

As you create these assignments, you need to keep in mind how much students will complete in class. Again, it is better to overplan than to underplan. One of the worst situations you can put a substitute in is having too little planned. Leaving students without any work to do for a long period of time is just a problem waiting to happen.

Even if students don't complete all of their work in class, you should require them to turn in what they have done to the substitute. This allows you to see if they actually worked during class. This is just another way to have some accountability for the students and the substitute. There is an example of a substitute lesson plan and a blank substitute lesson plan included on the CD that accompanies this book.

ALERT

Sometimes students will not turn in their work to a substitute for fear that it will be lost. However, this is not an excuse that you should accept. One of the only ways you can hold your students accountable is to see how much they completed while you were gone.

Emergency Lesson Plans

You should create a stock of emergency lesson plans in case you have to call in for a substitute at the last minute. These are usually left with the substitute coordinator in the office or with your fellow teachers. Make sure to leave the name of the person or people who have copies of your emergency lesson plans in your substitute folder.

Because you do not know when you will use them, emergency lesson plans will obviously not relate directly to what you are teaching at the time you will be out. Here are a few ideas for some emergency lesson plans:

- Questions from a chapter in the book that you are not planning to cover
- Worksheets that are self-contained
- Worksheets that might be considered interesting or fun, such as crossword puzzles
- Outside readings with questions

You don't know what your students will be scheduled to learn on these occasions, so stick with general activities that will give the substitute something educational to do with the students.

Scheduling Substitutes

Every school and district has a different system for scheduling substitutes. Some schools even require teachers to call and arrange for their own substitutes through a centralized district substitute bank. Make sure to learn the steps you must go through when you first begin teaching. It may be too late when you wake up early in the morning and discover that you're sick and need a substitute teacher.

ESSENTIAL

Ask veteran teachers about any advice they have concerning absences and arranging substitutes. Sometimes they will have insights that will allow you to better understand the system for scheduling substitutes and may be able to give you timesaving tips.

Act Early

If possible, do not wait to schedule your substitutes. As soon as you know you are going to be gone, make arrangements with your school. For example, if you have planned a field trip three months in advance, it is not too early to schedule a substitute for the students who will be left behind. There is a limit to the number of substitutes available. If the school district runs out of substitutes for a particular day, the teachers who got their requests in early will receive preferential treatment.

Temporary duty situations where you are doing something for the school are quite different from personal days you might take. Most districts have policies regarding appropriate uses of sick and personal days. Usually, this means that teachers cannot use these days for vacations. Instead, they are meant for situations when you truly are sick or when you have a doctor's appointment scheduled. Make sure you check your school district's policy concerning using these days before making plans.

Last-Minute Absences

Despite all your efforts, there will be times when you will need to call in at the last minute to get a substitute. Most schools and districts have a cut-off time by which you need to call. Hopefully, you will have a nice person who is in charge of answering the phones in the morning and who remembers that you are calling in because you are sick.

However, if the person is not particularly nice or caring, do not allow yourself to feel guilty for doing what is in your best interest. Remember, she is probably stressed too. You should make sure to stay polite and keep things on a professional level at all times. Remember, this person may be a huge help to you at some future point in your teaching career. (People in key positions will be discussed further in Chapter 18.)

FACT

Many districts do not allow you to call in sick the day before or the day after a holiday. This stops teachers who would abuse the privilege by taking an extra day of vacation. However, if you are truly sick, you should still request the day off.

Again, it is a good idea to have lesson plans prepared just in case you are going to be out. This is especially prudent if you are beginning to feel ill when you leave school at the end of a workday. If there is a chance you might take the next day off, go ahead and leave your lesson plans and substitute folder on your desk just in case. It is also a good idea to make sure the teachers around you and the substitute coordinator know where your substitute folder and emergency lesson plans are located.

Final Preparations

When you know you're going to be absent, you need to make sure that you inform your students. Go over your expectations for them in terms of work and behavior and reiterate that all work must be turned in to the substitute. It is also a good idea to tell your fellow teachers that you will be gone. That way they can help the substitute if there are problems.

It is important to double-check with the substitute coordinator before your absence and make sure that a substitute has actually been scheduled for your class. There is nothing worse than not getting a substitute. When this occurs, your students will usually be farmed out to your fellow teachers. This not only destroys your planned lessons but disrupts other teachers' lessons as well.

Finally, make sure that you have left your lesson plans and your substitute folder in full view on your desktop. And if you aren't confident the substitute will be able to find the folder or that it may go missing, leave the information with the teacher next door.

Student Behavior

Sometimes students who do not normally create problems in class will misbehave with substitutes. Therefore, it is very important that students understand you have high standards for their behavior. When you come back from your absence, make sure you do not ignore any behavioral problems that occurred while you were out.

QUESTION

What if a substitute gives a referral you disagree with?
In order to stay consistent, you must follow through with the referrals that substitutes turn into administration. However, if you truly feel that the referral was uncalled for, then you should discuss this with your supervisor.

Make Your Expectations Clear

You should hold your students to a high standard when you are absent. When a substitute is in your classroom, you want him to have a great day. For one thing, if he is a quality substitute, you will want him to return. For another, students need to understand that being rude to anyone is wrong. Students should realize that they will be punished if they misbehave.

Discipline and Rewards

When you state your expectations, you should make it clear what the consequences of misbehavior will be. You could choose to have students serve detention or write letters of apology to the substitute teacher. On the flip side, you should also provide rewards for exceptional behavior. Do this often at the beginning of the year and then periodically as the year progresses as a means of reinforcement.

Not All Substitutes Are Created Equal

There is a shortage of substitutes in many school districts across the nation, so quality standards are not always consistent across the board. You will have wonderful substitutes in your class, and you will have terrible ones. It is important that you take the time to inform your substitute coordinator or the central substitute office about exceptionally good substitutes as well as those who had problems.

FACT

There is a shortage of substitute teachers across the nation. Some states do not require that their substitutes be teaching certified. Others have resorted to increasing wages or actively recruiting substitutes through the Internet and newspaper advertisements.

What to Expect

You should expect your substitute to keep the class under control while implementing your lesson plan. However, sometimes you will find that the substitute placed in your class does not do one or both of these very well. She might have a real problem with classroom control. Or she might have been successful at making the students behave while failing to follow the lesson plan you provided.

It's understandable that many substitute teachers have problems with student behavior. However, there is a difference between minor misbehaviors and neglect. You should be really concerned if students come to class the next day and report behavior that could have led to student injury or simply indicates neglect on the part of the substitute teacher.

You will also find that some substitutes do not follow your lesson plans. Problems can range from minor errors to completely disregarding your instructions. As you leave instructions, be very careful to make things clear. Do not assume that your substitute knows what textbook your class is using. List the materials the substitute teacher should use, and leave reference copies if possible. Misunderstandings will occur and should be expected. However, if your substitute does not follow your lesson plan at all, you should definitely report this to the administration.

What to Do if Problems Occur

You should definitely report any serious concerns you have about a substitute teacher. Your school or district might have specific procedures you need to follow. Make sure that you are reporting the teacher for something important and not just a personality conflict.

In the end, realize that your students will probably not learn the same quality or amount of information during a day with a substitute as they would with you. This is not the fault of the substitute but the nature of the system. Because students know they probably will not be seeing a substitute again for some time, they feel they have more freedom to misbehave or simply ignore instructions. And there is the tendency for students to feel that work given by substitutes is mainly busy work. By creating realistic expectations, your substitute and students will have a successful experience during your absence.

CHAPTER 17

Meeting Diverse Needs

It is your first day of school. You enter your classroom to find one student who is gifted/learning disabled, one student who has cerebral palsy and is in a wheelchair, one who has serious visual learning disabilities, and twenty-seven who do not need special accommodations. As the teacher, you will be expected to teach all of the students in your class. This chapter should help to familiarize you with terms and issues you will face each day as a teacher of special-needs students.

Learning the Lingo

One of the biggest obstacles for new teachers is to get used to the language of disabilities. Much of the way that educators speak is through acronyms and citations of specific laws that have been passed. Even terms that you might think you understand often need further clarification when dealing with students with disabilities. You should learn the information presented here in order to be better prepared to handle your first individual education plan (IEP), staffing, and much more.

ESSENTIAL

Special education has so many acronyms that it often seems like alphabet soup. In fact, there are easily over 100 acronyms used by special educators. It is a good idea to use a reference guide if you are going to be in communication with special educators on a regular basis.

Acronyms for Short

You will hear your fellow teachers and other educational specialists use a number of acronyms. Some individuals will make sure that everyone understands what is being said, but others will not take the time to explain what each acronym stands for, so it's good to know what they mean. The following are some of the most common acronyms and their meanings:

IEP: Individual education plan
IDEA: *Individuals with Disabilities Education Act*
LD: Learning disabled
ESE: Exceptional student education
ADD/ADHD: Attention deficit disorder/attention deficit hyperactive disorder
ADA: *Americans with Disabilities Act*
ESL: English as a second language
LEP: Limited-English proficient
LRE: Least restrictive environment
FAPE: Free appropriate public education

If you ever hear an acronym or term that you don't understand, don't be afraid to speak up and ask what it means. It is better to look like you care enough to know than to pretend you understand and potentially get into trouble for not acting accordingly.

In addition to a variety of acronyms, you will also hear terminology that may be confusing. For example, you now know that LRE stands for "least restrictive environment," but you may not know what that means. LRE means full inclusion, or mainstreaming, and includes the idea that a student with a disability should be placed in a classroom with nondisabled classmates.

Individuals with Disabilities Education Act

The purpose of the *Individuals with Disabilities Education Act (IDEA)* is to allow those students who have disabilities to acquire the same level of education as students without disabilities. To achieve this, students are to be placed in the least restrictive environment (LRE). Further, each student is required to have an individual education plan (IEP) that would lead to substantive learning. Rules surrounding the IEP are discussed in the next section.

FACT

In the school year 1976–1977, fewer than 1 million students were served under IDEA. By 1999–2000, over 5 million students received these services. The increase is attributed to the increased number of students being classified as learning disabled. There are various reasons for this, but is due, in part, to improvements in diagnosing students who might have disabilities.

IDEA also makes some important demands concerning disciplinary actions against students with disabilities. These provisions apply both to students with physical and behavioral disabilities. Overall, the provisions of IDEA have a huge impact on schools and teachers.

Impact on the Teacher

IDEA will impact you as a teacher in many ways. For one thing, full inclusion means that you might be faced with the situation described in the beginning of this chapter. You will have to meet the needs of any students with disabilities in your classroom while teaching the rest of the class. Sometimes these accommodations will be as simple as providing the student with a written copy of any oral notes, and sometimes they will be more complicated. All of the accommodations are found on the IEP (as explained in the following section).

ESSENTIAL

Working with special-needs students may make you feel like you are being pulled in many directions, making it impossible to meet the needs of all your students. Keep a positive attitude, and set high expectations for yourself and your students. Remember that the IEP is a legal document that must be followed.

Many school districts provide teachers with classroom assistance for specific purposes. For example, some classrooms provide paraprofessionals who work with a specific group of students and aid the teacher in accommodations. Some school districts provide a certified special education teacher to co-teach with a regular education teacher. Other school districts might institute pull-out programs in elementary grades where students spend most of their time in the regular classroom but are pulled out for specialized instruction one or two days a week. You can learn more about pull-out programs later in this chapter. You might also find that your school district provides none of these but has the special education department provide support when you need it. For example, they might allow the disabled student to take a test with the special education teacher who can make additional accommodations.

Impact on Discipline

Disabled students fall under a different set of disciplinary guidelines. This is because some misbehavior can be directly related to their disability.

For example, if a student has Tourette's syndrome, she cannot be disciplined for cursing in class, as this behavior is a result of her disability. Enforcing discipline is especially problematic with students who have behavioral disabilities such as ADD, ADHD, and bipolar disorder.

Still, school officials do have the ability to ensure that the learning environment is safe. Therefore, students with disabilities can be removed from class if they pose a danger or violate the student code of conduct. However, school officials must follow specific rules regarding types and lengths of punishment for these students.

As the teacher, it can be hard to provide discipline for certain students. When you have a first grader with learning disabilities who continually "borrows" other students' items without returning them, helping him understand why his actions are wrong can be difficult. You will want to involve the special education resource teacher and the student's parents for help.

However, if you are faced with a severe discipline issue, you can still write referrals for these students. Just realize that the results of the referrals might not be what you had expected. Further, the special education teacher might contact you to work out a proactive behavior plan, which will hopefully minimize further behavior problems. Sometimes simply giving students with behavioral disabilities options and outlets can help them thrive in your classroom.

Problems arise when students with disabilities are temporarily removed from the school for disciplinary action. If the student is removed long enough that a "change in placement" occurs, then the school IEP team must determine how to continue serving the student in his new situation.

The Individual Education Plan

The IEP is a plan that must be followed by the school, special education staff, and regular teachers. The IEP results in increased accountability. If accommodations are not made according to the IEP, the school can be liable for disciplinary and legal actions.

Writing the IEP

When it becomes apparent that a student might have a disability, a staff meeting occurs and tests are administered to the student to determine if she is, in fact, disabled. Once a student has been identified as having a disability, she requires an IEP. An IEP team meets with parents and their advocate, if they desire, to formalize the IEP. According to the *IDEA Amendments of 1977*, a regular education teacher must be part of the IEP team.

The IEP that the team creates must include a statement of the child's current educational situation and a description of how it's affected by her disability. The IEP must also provide measurable annual goals for the child's education, the services that the special education department must provide, and the accommodations that must be made in the regular classroom.

ALERT

There is some concern that the nature of the IEP process is such that students from wealthier families tend to get the most services. Their parents often have the means to hire advocates to fight for their right to include as much as possible in the students' IEPs.

Part of the problem with IEPs is that they often serve as points of contention between parents and schools. Schools are liable to follow anything listed in the IEP, so they will work to make them as simple as possible. On the other hand, parents want the most for their children, so they will often fight to get as much included on the IEP as possible.

Teacher Accountability

It is imperative that you receive a copy of each disabled student's IEP and read through it completely. If you have any questions about the provisions of the IEP, you need to ask a special education specialist before the year begins. Remember, if you do not follow the provisions of the IEP, you and your school district can be sued. Therefore, make sure that you follow the IEP and that you keep detailed records concerning compliance. Then, if a problem should arise, you will have your records to show how you made the required accommodations.

Inclusion in the Classroom

According to the law, a student with a disability must be placed in the least restrictive environment possible and should only be removed from the regular classroom if his disability is so severe that even with extra aid and help, the student cannot learn in that environment.

This means that even if you don't teach a special-needs class, you will have many students throughout your teaching career who are disabled in one form or another. Many of these students will have learning disabilities that will not be apparent, but others will have disabilities that are very apparent to the rest of your class.

Arguments for Full Inclusion

The idea of full inclusion is still considered controversial by some people. Proponents of full inclusion believe that this system is necessary to provide a free appropriate public education (FAPE) to all students. If learning-disabled students are not allowed to join the general school population, they will be missing out on the same education as those in the mainstream. Further, there will be a stigma associated with them for attending special classes, and they will never be able to feel as if they are really part of the school. Therefore, unless their disability precludes them from being able to learn in the normal classroom, they should be placed there.

ESSENTIAL

Courts have tended to agree with the idea of full inclusion. Many times, the courts have cited the importance of giving all students equitable education, along with the idea that all students will benefit from the addition of individuals with disabilities to the classroom.

Another reason for full inclusion is that regular students have the opportunity to see the special-needs students as part of their class. The hope is that the more nondisabled students are around those with disabilities, the less prejudice there will be against them. The interaction will help broaden the horizons of all students and lead to a better, more congenial educational experience for all. The different perspective of the students with disabilities will add to the class as a whole.

Arguments Against Full Inclusion

Those who are against the idea of full inclusion also have a range of arguments to support their opinion. For one thing, parents of disabled children sometimes fear that full inclusion will lead to less—not more—attention for their students. According to L. H. Cohen in *Train Go Sorry: Inside a Deaf World,* the deaf community is concerned that full inclusion places their language and culture at risk. Further, some advocates argue that the needs of highly gifted students cannot be met in the regular classroom.

Another argument used against full inclusion is that increased exposure of disabled to nondisabled students does not necessarily lead to greater acceptance. Instead, students with disabilities are faced with even greater amounts of prejudice and name-calling. This is especially true for students who are the slowest or the fastest learners.

When a teacher has to spend extra time making accommodations so that the students with disabilities understand a lesson, students without disabilities may complain and make the disabled students feel embarrassed. Similarly, when gifted students learn everything very fast, other students might make fun of them. While teachers can work against this, they are not always successful. Students may just wait until the teacher is not around or listening to make their comments.

Teaching Students with Diverse Needs

It is important that you face each class and situation with a positive attitude and make no distinctions between students with disabilities and the rest of the class. If you single out any of the students, your actions may result in prejudice and bad feelings among your students. Remember that you set the tone in your classroom, so teach by example.

Problems with Other Students

Despite your best efforts, you may face some problems with nondisabled students. Students can be cruel to each other, so it is important that you keep a constant handle on the situation in the classroom. All students need to feel that you welcome them to your room.

You might have a disabled student in your class with a problem that is very obvious to all students. For example, you might have a student with cerebral palsy who does not have the use of his arms or legs and who is confined to a wheelchair. It can be difficult to balance the needs of one person with the needs of many, but you need to work hard to accommodate all the students in your classroom. If you feel that a situation is getting out of hand, don't be afraid to ask for help. Sometimes the nondisabled students in your class might need extra counseling to help them relate to the disabled student.

QUESTION

What are accommodations and modifications?
An alteration in the way you teach your students is an accommodation. A modification, on the other hand, is a change in the expectations of what students are supposed to learn in a class.

Special Accommodations

All students are equal, but they are not the same. Each student's situation is different. You need to use the IEP as your guide because it is a legal document to which you will be held accountable. If you need help understanding or completing an accommodation, do not be afraid to turn to your special education department. The important thing is that you do your best and document your efforts.

Some common accommodations you will be faced with might include the following:

- Providing written copies of notes
- Providing extra time on assignments and tests
- Reading worksheets and test questions aloud
- Placing the student in preferential seating
- Allowing tape recordings of classroom information
- Allowing students to type their work

- Using modified standards for grades
- Sending home frequent progress reports

Obviously, you will need help with some of these accommodations. If you are giving students an exam and one student needs the test questions read out to her, you will require assistance from teachers in the special education department. Therefore, you need to work closely with them to make sure that all parts of the IEP are met.

Pull-Out Programs

Many elementary and some middle schools across the United States provide extra services to students through pull-out programs. In this way, the students are included in the traditional classroom the majority of the time but receive special services once or twice a week according to their personal needs. This situation creates unique challenges that teachers must deal with.

Types of Pull-Out Programs

There are numerous types of pull-out programs that exist across the nation. The types of programs you might encounter could include any of the following:

- Gifted Programs
- Speech Therapy
- Reading Support
- ESL Support
- ESE Support
- Voluntary Music Programs
- Additional Specialized Pull-Out Programs

The number of days that the students are pulled out per week varies depending on the program and the school. In some cases, students might miss an entire day of class while in other schools they might be pulled out for one to two hours a few days a week. In any case, it is important to remember your students who are participating in pull-out programs as you create your lessons each week.

The Challenges Teachers Face

New teachers often find that dealing with class work and students who participate in pull-out programs can be challenging. If you have students who are missing an entire day of lessons each week, you will need to plan for this. You will need to avoid special activities that cannot be made up by students on their own. It would be unfair for those students to miss important or fun activities because they have to attend a pull-out program.

Deciding on lessons for pull-out days will also depend on the number of students affected and the number of times per week. For example, if five of your thirty students leave your class one day a week for a gifted program, then you will want to make sure that any work you cover can be easily explained through written notes or worksheets. At the same time, you will need to continue moving your lessons forward and covering necessary material with the other twenty-five students in your class. This can be a delicate balancing act. It's best to speak with other teachers at your school to find out how they make these programs as successful as possible for the students involved.

Working with a Co-Teacher

Some schools have a co-teach model for certain classes. In this model, two certified teachers are in the room at the same time. The co-taught class generally is made up of a larger percentage of students with disabilities than is normally allowed for one teacher. The regular teacher is in charge of the curriculum for the course. The special education teacher is in charge of all modifications and accommodations according to the IEPs.

Pros and Cons

There are pros and cons to this type of situation. On the positive side, regular teachers get extra help in their classroom for students with disabilities. The two teachers can work together to help reach all students in the classroom, a feat that is sometimes impossible for a teacher working by herself.

On the other hand, the benefits of having co-teachers are only achieved if the two teachers have a good working relationship. Unfortunately, two teachers may have conflicts over teaching philosophy and other issues. Further, even though most co-teachers in the classroom will make an effort to keep the identity of students with disabilities confidential, it is impossible for students not to realize who is and who is not being served by the co-teacher. This can best be combated by having the teacher help all students in specific ways to minimize singling out a certain student or group.

Communication and Cooperation

Because most of the issues between co-teachers stem from personality conflicts and lack of communication, it is imperative that co-teachers carry on open communication. If this is not the case, major problems are bound to occur.

As the regular education teacher, do not assume that the co-teacher is a threat or wants to take over your class. Further, never treat the co-teacher as if she were an aide. Remember, she holds a teaching degree, too. Make sure that you share your expectations concerning your students' education with the co-teacher. If you ever have any questions or concerns, do not be afraid to speak up. The co-teacher will probably make some accommodations that you might not agree with, but remember that both of you are constrained by the IEP.

In 1992, a jury in West Virginia awarded monetary damages to the parents of a special education student for the failure of teachers and a school to follow the IEP. This case, *Doe vs. Withers*, is important because the teachers who refused to implement the IEP were fined $10,000 each.

It's possible that you and your co-teacher won't get along. However, as professional educators, you must realize that you both want the same thing: a quality education for your students. You have to deal with each other and get along for the sake of your class.

CHAPTER 18

Walking the Staff Tightrope

As a teacher, you spend practically all of your time interacting with people. The majority of this time is spent in front of a class. In fact, sometimes you will feel like you rarely get to speak with other adults. However, it is very important that you spend some time building relationships with your school's administration and staff. These are the people who can either help to make your days better or make them much more difficult to bear.

Your Place as a New Teacher

You are in a unique position as a new teacher. The other teachers and people around you will probably have different ideas and concerns about you as you come into the school setting. Some veteran teachers might see you as a threat because you represent new ideas. This will especially be the case if you come into a staff meeting the first day and start speaking up about the ideas you want to implement. You might have some great ideas, but it would be wise to use a little tact and judgment before speaking with authority before a group of veteran teachers.

Other teachers will see you as someone to help. They may even try to mold you to their vision of what a good teacher should be. Be careful whose vision you follow, and make sure that it is consistent with your own beliefs. Just because someone who has been teaching for twenty years has a strong opinion regarding how you should teach does not mean you have to take this opinion at face value.

FACT

According to the U.S. Department of Labor, a large proportion of teachers are set to retire by 2010. Further, enrollments for students appear to be on the rise. This means that many vacancies in the teaching field are expected, and many new teachers will be entering the workforce each year.

Take Offered Help

Some teachers will try very hard to help you. It is advisable to take any offered help because it will only make your life easier. For example, if a teacher offers to help you create a rubric for an upcoming assignment, do not turn it down. He may have years of experience to offer as well as some real insight into making this activity more successful.

Similarly, if there is a teacher on your staff who is considered to be very effective, do not be afraid to ask for advice. When you get it, pay close attention. You might find insights that will help you accomplish your goal of being an effective teacher.

Avoid Too Many Extra-Duty Situations

New teachers are often hoodwinked into getting involved in many projects. Veteran teachers are often overworked and involved in other projects, so they just do not have the time to participate in one more thing. However, if possible, you should avoid getting too involved during your first year.

Do not volunteer for every duty that comes along, but be smart and get involved with those that will give you the most reward for your time. This might sound mercenary, but you are the only person who will look out for your own best interest. (More will be said about this in Chapter 19.)

Keeping People Happy

While it is important to work toward building strong relations with everyone on your staff, you need to realize that there are some people who can really help make your time teaching more profitable and enjoyable. Therefore, it is important to know who you should spend some extra time getting to know.

Obviously, you will want to get along with as many people as you can in your teaching job in order to create a happy work environment for yourself. The focus on specific individuals in this chapter is meant to highlight those individuals who can have a significant impact on your day-to-day job. When you build good relations with key people, you will find that they will bend over backward to help you out.

Administration

It goes without saying that when you first begin teaching—and throughout your career—you need to keep your bosses happy. They are the ones who control whether you will be hired each year. They are also responsible for dispersing teaching assignments, which can make your life easier or more difficult.

Many times, new teachers get the most difficult schedules, which often include multiple preps. If you are seen as a hard worker and a team player, it's hoped that the administration will do its best to lighten your load as soon as they can. However, if you cause them problems or are difficult to work with, they will be much less likely to look for ways to reward you.

When you are dealing with the school administration, there will probably be varying personalities at play. You should focus on the assistant principal directly in charge of you along with the principal of the school. These two people are most likely to influence decisions about your future.

ALERT

At many schools, the administration is seen as having an adversarial role in its relationship with the teachers. This is especially compounded when a former teacher becomes an administrator. This situation does not have to be the case if lines of communication are kept open.

Office Staff

While the administration is important for the big decisions, like making teaching assignments, the office and administrative staff are much more important on a day-to-day basis. The people in the office that you need to make sure and build relationships with are these:

- The principal's secretary
- The bookkeeper
- The substitute coordinator
- The registrar
- The benefits coordinator

Each of these people can help make your life easier as the year goes on. The principal's secretary controls your access to the principal. This is important if you want to be able to discuss something with the principal.

The bookkeeper is important because you will be dealing with him in a variety of ways throughout your career. You will probably be collecting money at some point for field trips or as a club sponsor. This money gets turned into the bookkeeper at the end of each day. By keeping this individual happy, you are going to make this time-consuming occurrence much more pleasant. Further, if you make mistakes, you will be much more likely to be quickly forgiven and gain needed assistance.

The substitute coordinator is very important because she controls who gets placed in your class when you are sick. Make sure that you know the procedures so that you can follow them to the letter. If you are on good terms with the substitute coordinator, you are more likely to get your requests put through for specific substitutes. You will also probably be treated better when you do have to call in sick.

The registrar can be important when it comes time to turn in grades. He is also the person who handles grade changes in the unlikely event that a mistake is made. While you might not be dealing with this individual on a day-to-day basis, it is a great idea to build a good relationship here. That way, when you do have a request, it will be dealt with quickly.

The benefits coordinator is an important person at your school because she can help you when important decisions come up. She will probably be the person you will get in touch with if you are hurt. She will also be your first point of contact when you have questions about your benefits.

FACT

The purpose of building relationships should be more than just trying to get special favors. The relationships you build could lead to lifelong professional and personal friendships.

Support Staff

Other members of the staff are also important to your career as a teacher. The most important are the media center or library personnel, the technology coordinator, and your custodian. The media center personnel are important because they are in charge of scheduling time in the media center. If you have a good working relationship with these individuals, you will be given more leeway. Part of building this relationship is to be on top of discipline issues while in the media center. If you show that you are trying to keep your students under control, you will be rewarded with preferential treatment above those teachers who do not watch their students carefully.

Technology coordinators are important because they control the borrowing of technology at the school. They usually have a central location where all equipment is stored. If you have a strong relationship with these people, you will find that it is easier to get the items you need when you need them. Further, they will be more likely to keep you in mind as they order new software and hardware.

One final individual that you really need to take some time getting to know is your custodian. Usually a good relationship means a better job cleaning your room. Many of these hard-working individuals are not given the respect they deserve. If you treat them well, you will be well rewarded.

Following the Chain of Command

One of the first things that you should learn when you begin a new teaching assignment is your chain of command. In other words, find out the name of not only your direct supervisor, but that person's direct supervisor as well, and so on, all the way to the principal. Once you know what your chain of command is, you can follow it when you have issues or problems. If you do not follow this chain, you will quickly cause problems for yourself.

For a Very Good Reason

Following the chain of command is important because you work more closely with those supervisors directly above you than with those at the top. If you have a problem, you should discuss it with your direct supervisor first. This gives your supervisor the opportunity to resolve your problem without sending it any further up the chain of command. If you do not allow your supervisor to at least try and resolve your issue, you are sending a message that you do not trust that he will do what is in your best interest. This proverbial "slap in the face" will lead to hard feelings when the person above your supervisor reports back to him and asks why he did not solve your problem before it got escalated.

If you go to your direct supervisor and she ignores your problem, then you have full rights to go to her supervisor. However, you should realize that when you do, you will probably cause some hard feelings with your supervisor. Make sure that the issue you are dealing with is truly an important one that justifies going further up the chain of command.

When Not to Follow the Chain

With that said, there are times that you should not follow the chain of command. For example, if you have an ethical issue dealing with your direct supervisor, it only makes sense to go directly above him with the problem. Similarly, if each member of your administration has different focuses, you would go directly to the individual who is in charge of the area where you have a concern. For example, if you have a testing issue, you would go to the assistant principal in charge of testing, instead of your direct supervisor. In the end, it's best to use your common sense when you are dealing with issues and problems to guide you to the correct person for your situation.

Making Good Colleague Choices

As many parents have said to their children, "You will be judged by your friends." Even if a child is a straight-A student who never gets into trouble, if she hangs out with criminals and drug dealers, she will be seen as a trouble-maker too. This principle also holds true for you in your professional career as a teacher. The only difference is that drug dealers would be replaced with disgruntled employees.

Don't misunderstand the point. You are not obligated to avoid certain teachers, and you should be polite to everyone. But take care choosing the teachers with whom you have strong friendships, because your friendships will be the measure many will use to judge you and your commitment to teaching. Following are some types of teachers that you might encounter as you teach.

The "Ready to Retire" Teacher

Teachers who are getting close to retirement will probably be the best teachers you will work with. They have years of experience and insight that they can share with you. They make the best mentors and should be sought out for advice. However, there are a couple of things you might want to consider when dealing with these teachers.

While excellent veteran teachers are common, you will probably also come into contact with those teachers who have the "ready to retire" mindset. These teachers are counting down the days until they reach twenty or thirty years of work and can retire from teaching altogether. These teachers are suffering from the educator's version of "senioritis": They are only paying attention partially to their work because they are ready for the end of the year.

ALERT

Just as in other areas of life, you must use your best judgment and common sense when those around you give advice. It is a good idea to take any concerns you might have to your mentor, team leader, or supervisor before following questionable advice.

Also, you might find "ready to retire" teachers who are somewhat disgruntled. Over the years, they have probably had to face many changes. If a new change occurs during their last years, they may see it as more of a nuisance than an opportunity. This negative attitude is catching and can deflate you very quickly.

The "Cavalier" Teacher

Some teachers just seem to have a cavalier attitude about their careers. Typically, they have been around for a while and choose to ignore or alter instructions given to them because they have taken the idea of "tenure" too far. They know that they cannot be fired if they do not step too far out of bounds. For example, this type of teacher might realize that since he gets his check by direct deposit, he can ignore any directives that say "You will not be paid on time if you do not . . . "

Often, teachers with this type of attitude are negative about any new or different ideas for education. They will put as little time as possible into changing. If you hang around those with a negative attitude, this will rub off on you. To maintain your positive outlook on teaching and students, it might be best to steer clear of these negative people.

The "Excited" Teacher

The excited teacher is a great person to spend time with. She will often be positive about her job and will be involved in her school. However, you should be careful that these individuals do not get you too deeply involved in any projects when you are new to the school. They have often been teaching long enough to feel confident in the classroom and to have all of their lessons in place. You, on the other hand, will require two to three years to become truly confident in your abilities and to have a good basis in your position. It's fine to become friends, but do not allow yourself to be pushed into more than you can handle.

The "Committed Realist" Teacher

This individual is very committed to his job, yet he is very realistic about the state of education and the school. While these individuals are sometimes seen as negative by administration, they often have the most stable view of what is really going on around you. Therefore, it is very good for you to get to know someone like this to help ground you in reality. However, realize that this could have some negative connotations for you. Use your common sense to judge if teachers like this are truly committed to providing an excellent education for their students.

The "Incompetent" Teacher

This last type of teacher is, hopefully, the one you will not encounter at all. This is the teacher who appears so incompetent that other educators doubt whether she can really teach. You will hear horror stories from other teachers and students about her classroom environment.

ALERT

You will encounter more good teachers than bad ones in your teaching career. When you work with someone who does a terrible job in the classroom, it is hard to keep quiet. However, you need to follow the chain of command when lodging complaints about these teachers.

It would be advisable not to take advice from the incompetent teacher. However, it is also a very good idea not to become involved in any discussions with students concerning her teaching skills. If you really feel that something terrible is happening in her classroom, discuss this with your team leader or your immediate supervisor.

Staff Gossip

The school campus is a prime place for gossip, and you'll be exposed to it as well. Many times gossip is told over lunch or during planning periods. The best advice you can get as a new teacher is: "Listen, smile, and move on." In other words, if you do not want to be rude and say something like, "Please do not gossip in front of me," just listen to what is said without making any judgments at all. Some of what you hear will be true, and some will be false. As a new teacher, you may not have all the background information to make the distinction between the two.

It is in your best interest not to spread gossip around. For one thing, as a new teacher you will not really understand all the inner workings of the staff. There might be teachers who once dated or teachers who are related to each other. If you repeat the wrong piece of gossip to the wrong person, it could really cause a problem. It is best if you just don't get involved.

Personality Conflicts

The odds are that you'll eventually encounter a colleague with whom you just cannot seem to get along. This person might be another teacher with whom you have little contact. However, it might also be someone more important to you, like your team leader or supervisor. The best thing you can do in this situation is to try harder to get along, even if it seems like you are doing all of the bending.

This does not mean that you should always give in or that you have to be this person's best friend. But it does mean that you should be friendly and look for ways in which you can be helpful. You might even find that you can build a good working relationship from a somewhat rocky start just by being the first to swallow your pride and move forward. Remember, your job and your time revolve around your attitude. If you approach each person and situation in a positive manner, you will have a much happier and enjoyable time as a teacher.

CHAPTER 19

Avoiding "New Teacher" Exploitation

As the newest member of the faculty, you may find that you are given less consideration than veteran teachers. You may not be given the best classes or the best duties to perform. In fact, many times you will feel that others are taking advantage of you just because you are new. Hopefully, you will find mentors and administrators who help you out. However, if this is not the case, you should understand the benefits of saying "yes," along with some reasons that you may be given less consideration and ways to say "no."

Positive Effects of Participating

First, it is important to point out that there are many positive aspects to happily participating in activities across the school. These effects are often intangible but can bring huge rewards over the long run. Before you start complaining about all the extra effort you have to put in when you should be focusing on your classroom teaching skills, take some time to consider the benefits of saying "yes."

Meeting Other Educators

By participating in committees and extracurricular activities, you will be able to meet other teachers with whom you might not otherwise have contact. Because of the solitary nature of teaching, it is often easy to stay isolated in your small space. However, meeting other teachers can have huge benefits for you.

ESSENTIAL

Begin building relationships with your coworkers from day one. A necessary part of a successful career is finding a network of friends and fellow teachers you can talk to and rely on.

You might also get to know administrators and staff members better. Being involved with them in less formal ways can help you build enjoyable and fruitful relationships with them. Further, meeting colleagues with different responsibilities and teaching personalities can help you grow as an educator.

Getting to Know the Students

When you get involved with clubs, sports, and other extracurricular activities, you can really get to know students. Building relationships can help you in your own classroom and also in the school at large. For example, if you are on duty in the lunchroom and a student from another class begins misbehaving, you will have a better chance of handling the situation if you actually know the student or her friends.

You will also find that many students are fun and interesting to be around. These students can make the extra hours of participation worth it. Getting to know them can help enhance your day-to-day teaching because they can provide you with feedback and insights that teachers don't normally get. Connecting with students can truly make the difference between being a success or a failure as a teacher.

Being a Team Player

If you are seen as a team player, you will find that even though you are given extra duties and work, you will also be given greater consideration in the future. For example, teachers who never get involved may find that their requests might be denied. However, administrators will often work out ways to grant requests for teachers who are part of the team.

Being a team player means that you will feel a greater sense of belonging to your school. If you feel that you are truly a part of the school, then being involved will have more appeal because you want your school to succeed in all endeavors. Remember, your attitude truly determines whether you see participation as a positive or negative experience.

Proving You Can Be Trusted

Keeping promises and showing that you are trustworthy is an important skill that you must nurture. Nothing can replace someone else's trust in your abilities and your word. Similarly, if you are not considered worthy of trust, you will find that many doors will be closed to you. Therefore, if you do become involved in something, give it your full attention. If you cannot give it your best effort, or you are not able to live up to your obligations because you are just working too much, go to your administrator and explain the situation. They will trust you more if you are honest with them than if you try to do something halfway and fail.

Your Teaching Assignment

Before you even begin working at your new school, much of what you will experience during your first year as a teacher has already been decided for you. Administrators make course and teacher assignments over the summer.

These decisions determine exactly what grade and classes you will actually teach. Because you are the newest addition to the school, you can expect that you will probably not be given the choicest assignments.

This does not mean that everyone is out to get you or give you the hardest work. However, realize that many teachers feel that they should be given the better assignments because they have worked their way up the seniority ladder. Also, remember that they probably started out teaching the less desirable assignments too.

One reason that new teachers do not always have the best luck with teaching assignments is because veteran teachers often have a say in what they are teaching each year. Many times, administration will ask members of a department to get together and give them a guide to who will be teaching what the following year. In most instances, teachers will continue to teach the same subject each year. However, if someone who has a "choice assignment" leaves or retires, the most senior teacher who wants to change assignments will get her courses. Then, the most senior below this individual can change his assignment, and so on. What this means for you is that those individuals who had the worst teaching assignments will move out of them as soon as they can, leaving them for the newest person on the staff.

ESSENTIAL

Don't expect to come into a school and teach your dream class right away. While you might dream of teaching only third grade or tackling AP American history, you might end up teaching in a different elementary grade or being assigned to courses like regular world history. Even though these assignments may not be what you envisioned, they can provide you with opportunities to learn and grow as a teacher.

Multiple Preps

One of the problems that many new secondary school teachers face is that they are given all of the leftover courses. For example, a new high school social studies teacher might have the following teaching schedule:

1. Planning period
2. Economics
3. World history
4. Honors economics
5. American history
6. Law studies

Teaching different courses is known as having multiple preps. If you teach five different courses, you have to prepare five sets of lessons each day. Obviously, this is not an easy situation to be in. You may think that a school should realize the obvious—that a new teacher has so many other issues to be concerned about, assigning her to teach five different subjects is just a recipe for disaster. However, the only way a school can remedy the situation is by forcibly moving veteran teachers who have been teaching their courses for a while out of their assignments in order to give the assignment to the new teacher.

Difficult Students

As a new teacher, you might be faced with the more difficult students in the school. While this does not happen everywhere, in many schools across the country teachers are able to influence who is and is not placed into their classrooms. Veteran teachers might be able to get a known troublemaker replaced with a better-behaved student. As a result, your classes could have a higher percentage of troublemakers than others.

ALERT

Approach each class as important. Some teachers treat regular and honors classes differently. However, do not shortchange the students who are earning a regular credit in your course. They need the information and skills that you will teach them as much as—if not more than—students in honors classes.

If you find that you have a large number of very difficult students in your classroom, do not be afraid to discuss this with your mentor and possibly your administrator. Sometimes administrators will separate students who have a hard time working with each other by removing one from your class. This may be enough to alleviate the situation and make your teaching experience much easier.

School Committees

Most schools have committees that require teacher participation. Usually teachers have to be a part of at least one committee, so you will probably be assigned to or asked to join a committee during your first week of school or even earlier. If you are assigned to a committee, then you just have to deal with whatever committee is given to you. However, if you are allowed to choose, realize that not all committees require the same amount of work. If you can, try to pull aside a veteran teacher and ask her opinion about each committee's workload. You may find that the Testing Committee requires many hours of work while the Technology Committee does not.

Even with this information, you may not get the assignment you ask for. If you can, limit your committee membership to just one committee. In other words, you might not be able to say "no" to two committees if asked, but do not volunteer to join a second committee.

ESSENTIAL

When making decisions concerning your career, it is a good idea to think in terms of the long run. Even though committees and other activities may seem trivial or even a nuisance, they can create situations that could lead you closer to your goals.

Once committee work begins, you may find that other members turn to you with extra work. While it is expected that as a committee member you will fully participate, you should speak with your committee leader if you feel that you are given the majority of the work. If you are very agreeable to everything without ever speaking up, you will be taken advantage of. This is especially the case if you are not only agreeable but also efficient. People who are known as hard workers usually get the most work.

However, if you do have the time and the interest to get involved, then you can make a real reputation for yourself at your school. If you have a goal to become an administrator, then you might want to consider joining a committee that gets you noticed. Committees vary in all schools, but some are more prestigious than others. These are the ones that wield more power in the day-to-day running of the school.

Extracurricular Activities

Another issue you may face is being asked to participate in extracurricular activities. This can be very hard for new teachers who are just trying to find their own teaching rhythm. Realize that you will probably be "required" to participate in some fashion. However, be careful to limit the number of activities you volunteer for based on all your other involvements and obligations.

Sponsoring a Student Club

Most schools have a large number of student clubs. Each year, new clubs arise and established clubs lose their adult sponsors. Therefore, you can expect that you will be approached at some point to become involved with a school club. Some clubs are much more time-intensive than others. For example, if you sponsor the school's chess club, all you may need to do is set up the chessboards and then enjoy the time with the students without a lot of effort on your part. However, service organizations like the National Honor Society and Interact often take a large amount of time and effort on the part of the adult sponsor.

Coaching a Sports Team

You might be asked to take part in your school's sports program. Your participation might be as simple as coming to the games to provide extra adult supervision, or it might be something more complicated like actually coaching a team. Being a coach of a team is often very time-consuming, although this depends on what sport you coach and the level of school participation. Certain sports have shorter seasons or less student participation or both.

However, coaching usually involves a supplement to your pay. With the relatively low salaries of teachers in most places, this extra income can be very nice. If your goal is to someday be a coach of a major sport, you will definitely want to volunteer and become involved.

Getting Involved with Other Activities

From time to time, your school will probably get involved in short-term initiatives or projects, and you may be asked to participate. For example, your school might have a history fair or a literacy week. You will probably be asked to help coordinate or assist in setting up these activities. Each activity that you participate in has a certain time commitment. Therefore, try to limit the number of activities that you become involved with. Because these are extra activities, it will probably be easier to decline the opportunity to participate.

FACT

The National Honor Society has rigorous qualifications for membership and lists obligations that members must meet in order to maintain their membership. The NHS chapter as a whole must complete a service project each year. All of this means more paperwork and time commitment from the teacher sponsor.

However, this may not be the case for "pet" projects specific to your school or community. For example, a rural school might be very involved with the state fair or have a weeklong festival that students consider a tradition. In these instances, you will probably be required to participate in some fashion as part of the faculty.

Additional Duties

As a new teacher, you may also be required to perform various duties around the school. For example, a "lunch duty" may require a teacher to sit out in the hallway or at a specified location to make sure that students at lunch do not disrupt other classes on campus. Some schools allow you to pick your duties, but others simply assign them.

If there are more duties than teachers to perform them, new teachers are often asked to take on extra duties. This can be very hard to refuse, especially if it's an administrator who's doing the asking. However, realize that if you happily accept these extra duties, you will be seen as a team player.

How to Say "No"

As a new teacher, you will probably be asked to do more than is humanly possible. When you find yourself completely overloaded, it is extremely important that you say "no" to some of the activities presented to you. Declining to participate can be difficult, but it is a skill just like any other you will learn as you teach.

The first thing you should remember is to pick and choose wisely. Think about your preferences and your goals. If you wish to become involved in the running of the school, become involved in a greater number of committees and activities that affect the school itself. If you are more interested in building relationships with students, spend your time participating in clubs, sports, and extracurricular activities.

When you have determined that you cannot add any more to your plate, politely decline any invitations to participate in any other activities, unless you are doing it as a personal favor to someone. When you say "no," explain your reasons. List what you are already involved in and why you do not feel that you can give the activity the time it deserves. By saying that you feel the activity is worthwhile and you do not want to shortchange it, you are not dismissing the value of the activity. Instead, you are saying that you just do not have the time.

ESSENTIAL

In every situation, use your best judgment. Choose your actions and activities wisely. Be tactful when accepting or declining additional responsibilities. Be enthusiastic in participation. A little common sense and courtesy go a long way.

If you do not feel comfortable with a firm "no," you could offer your services in a limited capacity. For example, instead of being the sponsor of a club, you could provide supervision or participate in one event. This shows the person involved that you are willing to help and be a team player.

In the end, you have to take care of yourself. Teachers who demonstrate good work will be asked to take on extra duties. New teachers may also be taken advantage of because others on the staff do not have the time or desire to become involved.

CHAPTER 20

The Pendulum Swing of Reform

Many people complain about the state of education today, and some are working hard to correct what they believe are the problems. Every year, new ideas are hatched and old ideas are dusted off in the hopes that they will fix the problems in education. As you teach, you will probably be faced with changes through reform measures every couple of years. It is in your best interest to accept change while continuing to use your best practices to give your students a quality education.

Cyclical Reforms

You will probably find that reforms change in a cyclical nature over time. What was once out of favor is now the hottest reform around. Many veteran teachers meet the latest reform ideas with skepticism because they have already experienced a previous version of that reform firsthand. The truth is that reforms in and of themselves will not change the issues with education. No matter what educational system a school adopts, only parents and teachers working together can actually make a difference.

Reforms come in many varieties. Schools may try to restructure their programs through various reforms, such as placing a greater emphasis on cooperative learning, using alternative assessments as opposed to traditional tests to determine grades, or grouping students by ability instead of age in the lower grades and by career opportunities or interests in the higher grades. Schools also have invested a great deal of effort and money reorganizing class schedules. They have manipulated the length of class periods and have changed the entire calendar in an attempt to give students a better educational experience.

ALERT

Realize that the field of education is always going through changes. Many teachers are fearful of change and do not want to move out of their comfort zone. If you would like to learn how to alter the way you look at change, read *Who Moved My Cheese?*, by Spencer Johnson, MD.

Reducing class size is one reform that many schools have not been able to try because of budget constraints. Despite the evidence that smaller classes can be more effective, it is difficult to get the funding to build extra schools, hire new teachers, and run the facilities each day.

Some educational reformers have decided to shift the emphasis from fixing public education to providing students with opportunities to leave public schools through a voucher program. It's believed that this will help eliminate the funding issues while giving students more choices and control over their education.

Changes in Classroom Procedures

Many reforms, whether encouraged or mandated, affect your methods of teaching and grading your students. These changes in classroom procedures are usually an attempt to move away from the traditional idea of education: a teacher lecturing and then testing students on the material. Some schools simply encourage teachers to alter and vary their instruction and assessment tactics. Others schools, however, place a lot of emphasis on completely revamping teaching methods and ideas.

Cooperative Learning

Cooperative learning is an educational method in which students work in small groups to complete assignments and other tasks. Cooperative learning works most effectively under the following conditions:

- Students are given assignments that work better when completed as a group.
- Groups are small, with three to five members.
- Assignments require students to work together.
- Each student is graded individually based on the effort made and how much he learned.

Unfortunately, one or more of these important points are often missing from cooperative learning assignments, thereby causing problems for teachers and students.

ESSENTIAL

Cooperative learning skills are very important in the business world today. Once students leave school and begin their careers, many will have to be able to work in teams to complete complicated projects.

Schools that stress the importance of cooperative learning over other methods of teaching may provide teachers with in-service support and hold meetings to discuss methods for implementation. These schools will try to reinforce the cooperative learning philosophy with teachers who depend too heavily on lecturing.

The value of varying your instruction in building interest and reaching students with different learning styles was discussed in Chapter 10. By varying instruction, you wisely choose the best method of instruction for each lesson that you create. Not every assignment or lesson lends itself to cooperative learning. Therefore, try to not only vary your instruction but to have valid reasons supporting your methods of instruction for each lesson.

Alternative Assessments

Alternative assessments require students to create a response, rather than having them choose the correct answer from a list. In the simplest terms, having students complete short-answer questions or write essays (as opposed to answering multiple-choice questions) is a form of alternative assessment. However, when most educators think of alternative assessments, they think of more complicated methods like oral presentations, projects, and portfolios.

Some schools have begun stressing these latter forms of alternative assessments, especially the use of projects and portfolios. For example, some schools have begun requiring seniors to complete a senior project before graduating. Other schools require teachers to collect a portfolio of work from students over time and use this to assign holistic grades based on content and improvement.

Ability Grouping

There has been a movement in some school districts to group students in elementary and middle schools according to their ability and not according to their age. Methods of grouping students vary; usually, school records and test scores are the main factors for forming student groups. Ability-grouping reforms are based on the belief that students who are advanced in math should be with other advanced math students. Similarly, those students who are working below grade level should be grouped together.

There is a difference between ability grouping and tracking. Ability grouping places students in a class based on their skill and achievement level instead of their age. Tracking places students of the same age or grade level in different levels of courses.

Advantages of Reform

The goal of this reform is to give students exactly what they need and not arbitrarily group them because they all happen to be the same age. If used correctly, this method allows teachers to create curriculum to directly meet the needs of their students. Advanced students will not get bored with easy classes and unchallenging material, while students who are getting behind will get the extra help they need.

Disadvantages of Reform

Obviously, the advantages to a well-developed system of ability grouping are huge. In fact, research shows that an effective program has positive effects on student self-esteem and performance. However, the disadvantages to this system must be addressed.

First, teachers must create different curriculum units for the different classes so that the high achievers will continue to be challenged. Further, if ability grouping is instituted across grade levels, the difference in ages of the students in a class can be significant. If a very advanced first grader can work at a sixth-grade math level, should she be placed in a group that has a different maturity level, where she might find it hard to be accepted?

Finally, it can be difficult to control the progression of students through the school. For example, you may have a third-grader who has completed all levels of math offered in the school but is still reading at a second-grade level. Do you create new math classes for that student? Do you send him to middle school for math and have him stay in elementary for the rest of his courses? These types of questions are not easy to answer because of the way that most schools in America are presently organized and the way that most educators presently think.

Interest and Career Grouping

Another method for reorganizing students focuses on looking at their interests and future career expectations. Sometimes students are moved into "learning communities" within their schools to focus their education around their interests. For example, some students might be housed as a "health" learning community. Courses would incorporate themes that would benefit students who might someday go into careers dealing with health.

In other areas, magnet schools have been created to attract students with similar interests. For instance, a performing arts magnet school might provide students with greater instruction and performance opportunities. Classes are taught keeping this focus in mind.

FACT

An early precursor to the magnet school began as an experiment in Minneapolis, Minnesota, in 1970. The city opened four elementary schools and one high school based on different organizational structures, including an open school, a traditional school, and a continuous progress school.

The Purpose of These Reforms

The purpose of grouping students by interest is obvious. Students will have greater buy-in regarding their education if they feel that it is truly focused on their likes and desires. Obviously, they will have to learn core subjects; however, students also spend time learning information that is useful in preparing them for later life. Further, educators do not have to use the "one-size-fits-all" method of education. They can frame their lessons around interest-building ideas related to the concerns of their students.

Challenges to Be Met

Grouping students by interest level within a school is a great challenge for educators. The idea of "schools-within-schools" has some definite physical advantages: Students get the benefits of this interest focus, but they share the same facilities. However, challenges arise when students do not stay within their "house" or "community." For example, there may be a performing arts community and a health sciences community at the same school, and some students who are in the health community might want to be involved in the band. This may make it difficult to determine where the band fits.

Further, if schedule conflicts prevent students from being placed in completely exclusive community classes, teachers will not be able to focus their lessons on that one interest group. As a core curriculum teacher, it can be difficult to teach a class that has students from three different communities. Students will also lose out on the original purpose of communities: placing students with similar interests together.

It can also be difficult for teachers to be part of more than one community at a school. This puts them in the situation of having to create different curricula based on the interests of students in those communities.

Magnet schools have their own share of problems. For one thing, there is concern about the equality of education. Some schools are better than others or receive more funding. And the quality of educators may not be the same.

Further, funding itself can cause problems because magnet schools, if created correctly, will not always contain the same number of students. In other words, the same number of students will not be interested in careers in health as will be interested in careers in the performing arts. Therefore, this imbalance can lead to wasteful spending and duplication of effort.

Block Scheduling

Block or modular scheduling involves restructuring the school day or week so that students are in classes for longer stretches of time. Numerous types of block schedules exist. A modified block schedule typically works within the normal context of the school week. In some instances, classes are longer on some days and are shorter or aren't taught at all on other days. Here is one example of a modified block schedule:

Day	Periods	Duration of Period
Monday	1–6	50–55 minutes
Tuesday	1, 3, 5, and 6	80 minutes
Wednesday	1, 2, 4, and 6	80 minutes
Thursday	2, 3, 4, and 5	80 minutes
Friday	1–6	50–55 minutes

According to this schedule, students meet only four times in a week for any given class, although the instructional teaching time remains the same. Likewise, teachers have only four planning periods in a week. However, the amount of planning time remains the same.

The 4×4 Block Schedule

A more radical block schedule is the 4×4 block. On this schedule, students complete a few classes very quickly. For example, students might take only four classes each term with 100-minute periods. Semester and year-long classes are completed in half the time, so students could conceivably complete sixteen semester classes or eight year-long courses each year.

Arguments for the Block Schedule

There are many good arguments that proponents use to support implementation of block schedules. For one thing, students have longer periods of time in class with each teacher, facilitating cooperative learning and longer science labs. Teachers have more flexibility in their planning. They can create more complicated assignments than they could normally teach in one traditional period. Teachers also have longer stretches of planning time in which to prepare better lessons.

Since fewer students are seen each day, and teachers are with the students they see for longer stretches of time, they are able to spend more quality time with the class. Students have less information to deal with each day and less homework on any given day during the week. It is also easier to spend extra time with students with disabilities because more time is available.

Arguments Against the Block Schedule

On the flip side, opponents argue that there are some major problems with the block schedule. For one thing, students who miss one day actually miss two in terms of class time. In a 4×4 block, if a student misses a week because of illness, she has actually missed two weeks' worth of material. This can be difficult for students to make up.

Opponents also point out that just changing the time spent in each class will not solve the problems with education. Even though students are in class the same amount of time under a block and a traditional schedule, student attention spans are such that it can be very hard to sit still for eighty or 100 minutes.

While the block schedule does lend itself well to varying instruction, the truth is that many teachers do not use the full amount of time. In effect, this counteracts one of the main benefits of the block schedule. In many instances, the extra time at the end of the class is left for students to do homework. Therefore, students could end up learning less and not more.

ALERT

Changing a school to a block schedule has a huge impact on education, and many educators will feel very passionate about this issue, whether they support or oppose it. As a new teacher, it is wise to be tactful about expressing your opinions on this issue.

The most compelling arguments against block schedules discuss the studies that have been done in schools using this system. One study completed by the Texas Education Agency in 1999 found that there was little evidence to support the claim that the block schedule results in increased student learning. Further, a study completed in 2002 by Iowa State University in conjunction with ACT, Inc., showed a potential correlation between block scheduling and decreased ACT scores. Clearly, more work needs to be done to prove the effectiveness of block scheduling.

Year-Round Education

When public education was first instituted in the United States, the country was basically agrarian. In the summer, children were required to work at home on the farm. Therefore, schools would let out for the summer and begin again after the harvest.

Some educators today argue that this system should be abandoned with the changing times and instead move to a year-round system of education. This does not mean students would go to school for a longer period of time. However, the vacations would be broken up differently so there would be no long summer vacation.

The most common scheme for doing this is the "45–15 Plan," where students go to school for forty-five days (eight weeks) and then have fifteen days (three weeks) off. Normal holiday breaks are still built in the calendar. Of course, there are other ways to divide the year.

The Benefits of Year-Round Education

Proponents of year-round education cite many reasons why it is an effective way to structure the school year. For one thing, students tend to forget a lot of what they learned over the lengthy summer break. As a result, teachers spend a long time at the beginning of each new school year reviewing information from the previous year's classes. This time would not be necessary in a year-round system of education. Short breaks could even be used to provide students with periods of enrichment education.

Other advantages are more practical in nature. For one thing, this system allows for a more efficient use of school facilities. Schools would not be closed for two to three months in the summer and allowed to become musty, leading to health concerns. Furthermore, a year-round system allows for vacation planning at any convenient time for the family. Finally, the year-round system is already used in much of the world.

QUESTION

How many U.S. schools have moved to year-round education?
Each year, the number of schools that implement year-round education around the nation is increasing. In 1990–1991, the number of schools that were using year-round education was 859. In 2002–2003, the number increased to 3,181.

It's Not as Great as It Might Sound

Many opponents of year-round education are those who work with sports and other extracurricular activities. They are concerned that students in band and chorus would have to work around the schedule for performances and competitions. Athletes would probably have to continue sports practice during three-week breaks and miss out on vacations altogether.

And the problem is not limited to musicians and athletes. Students who wish to have a summer job or participate in summer camps could be adversely affected by this system.

There is no conclusive evidence one way or the other whether year-round education is better for learning. The fact is that students are going to forget information during breaks, even if they are only three weeks long. Some educators claim that in a year-round system, they spend even more time reviewing concepts that are in danger of being lost because of the three-week breaks.

Setting Up Smaller Schools

Studies have shown that smaller schools increase student learning. They also lead to less violence and disruptive behavior, higher graduation rates, and increased student and teacher satisfaction. The reasons for this are varied. At least one factor is a more collegial feel among teachers who can work more closely and have the opportunity to form better relationships with students.

FACT

Opinions vary concerning the optimal size for schools. Some people believe that middle schools should be no larger than 400 to 500 students. The prescriptions for high schools range all the way from 300 to 1,500 students; most educators believe that between 600 and 1,000 students is a good number.

Funding is the problem in creating smaller schools. Unfortunately, many school districts do not have the money to build extra schools or divide huge campuses into smaller schools. Having a high school with 2,000, 4,000, or even 5,000 students is more cost-efficient than having several schools of 1,200 students each. When school districts do make the decision to create smaller schools, they often have to give up things such as music and enrichment classes. Making this choice is very difficult. Until funding methods change or people are willing to spend more in taxes to support schools, this will continue to be an issue.

Voucher Reforms

Vouchers are basically scholarships given to students so that they can go to a private school instead of their local public school. The arguments for vouchers are many. For one thing, people argue that schools will be forced to raise their standards in order to retain students if enrollment begins to decline. Further, vouchers provide lower-income students the opportunity to attend private schools that they might not be able to afford. Vouchers give these students more choice and control over their education.

The arguments for vouchers rely at least partly on the belief that public schools are failing. However, some people believe that the schools themselves are not the problem—it's the lack of support from community and parents for teachers and the schools that is really at issue. One reason that many private schools succeed where public schools fail is their greater incidence of parental involvement with students and school activities. Just giving students vouchers would not fix the problems themselves.

There is also a concern that if the state gives students vouchers to attend private schools, it might be seen as supporting religion. In other words, if a student chooses to use public funds to go to a Christian school instead of public school, taxpayers are paying for that student's education, which will likely include religious instruction. Whether or not this violates the First Amendment to the Constitution depends on who is reading the Constitution. Ultimately, the Supreme Court will be the judge of this issue.

CHAPTER 21

Thinking about Education in a New Way

What is the purpose of education in America? What constitutes a quality education? These are tough question with different answers depending on who is asked. Some might say that the point of education is to teach children the basics of reading, writing, and arithmetic along with a foundation in shared beliefs and values. However, a growing number of individuals have begun questioning and rethinking the American educational system. Today's world is much different than even thirty years ago, and this new landscape requires changes in the way we approach education.

Educational Theories of the Past

Despite all the talk and spending on new technologies and programs, the day-to-day methods by which students work and learn have not varied that radically since the early twentieth century. While there is more technology and a greater emphasis on cooperative learning, educational expectations of schools and students are largely unchanged. A student enters a grade, works through a standardized curriculum, memorizes a lot of information, passes both informal and formal assessments showing her knowledge, and then moves on to the next year. Talk to an older person about his educational experiences, and you might be shocked at how similar this is to what he experienced.

FACT

In the 1920s and 1930s, educational reformer John Dewey espoused a view that might be familiar to many teachers today. He claimed that education that was strict and authoritarian without making connections to the students' experiences was a major problem with schools. Teachers must make these connections to keep students interested.

The question that needs to be answered is: Does the old method of education make sense and actually work in today's world? Many would argue that the answer to this question is an emphatic no. The future of education needs to be adaptive, interactive, relevant, and challenging. Only by rethinking the entire educational system can you get to a point where this becomes reality.

Revisiting the Purpose of Education

In order to create a better educational system in America, one must revisit the purpose of education. Obviously, students need to learn to read, write, and solve math problems. But beyond that, why should children go to school? Is it to give them something to do? To prepare them for the workforce? To create leaders and thinkers? The answer to these questions holds the key to how schools should work.

Young people who leave school today need to have key skills that many employers and colleges say they are lacking. For one thing, many professions today stress the team concept. However, the skills necessary to work and produce as a team are often lacking in new graduates. Further, business owners also cite a greater need for problem-solving skills. The fact is that many students graduate without the necessary skills to analyze a problem and come up with possible solutions on their own. These two types of skills are not things that can simply be learned by rote. Instead, they must be modeled and experienced multiple times by students.

The education of the future has to produce students able to work independently or in a team environment. They must be problem solvers and critical thinkers. They must know how to go about learning something new. The majority of facts that students are required to memorize each day in the classroom will not be remembered two weeks later, let alone ten years later. However, if you can teach students the skills to acquire new knowledge on their own and use it to come up with novel solutions to problems they are experiencing, then you have truly done your job as an educator.

This does not mean that content is not important or should not be taught. Students need to learn content from a wide variety of curriculum areas for many reasons. They need to have a shared understanding and background. And even if students are not going to remember the first sixteen elements of the periodical chart, for example, the act of learning them in the first place is very important. With this they will gain an understanding of the periodical chart, its layout, and the elements themselves. When confronted with references to this in future years, they will be able to draw on this foundation of knowledge.

Adaptive Education

For education to work, it has to adapt to the individual student. Instead of focusing on the number of hours a student is in a class, you should be focusing on how well she has mastered the information. Unfortunately, the educational system is created so that a student moves along in lock-step with others through the years. However, some students learn faster and some slower. The fast ones often get bored and the slow ones often get lost.

In many cases, teachers are asked to determine on their own how to deal with students learning at different rates. They are expected to meet the needs of all the students in their class, no matter where they are in the curriculum. However, this can be very difficult when dealing with twenty-five to thirty students, daily disruptions, standardized test instruction, and so much more that is thrown their way. If, instead, system-wide changes were made whereby students would progress through grades based on what they have learned and not what grade they are supposed to be in, then you could truly be giving students an individualized and more effective experience.

ALERT

Student retention is often a hot-button political issue. The practice of promoting students to the next grade without passing the current one is called "social promotion." Neither retention nor social promotion is a perfect solution to low performance. It's important to learn your school's policy for retention and promotion.

Interactive Education

An effective system of education would provide students with a high level of interactivity. Instead of passive recipients of information they are expected to learn, students should be an integral part of lessons from the beginning. For example, instead of simply teaching students about a topic, a teacher might present students with a challenge that can only be solved by learning about and applying key information. In this way, students learn by helping to frame their experience.

Making It Relevant

Many teachers attempt to make connections between what students are learning and their own day-to-day experiences. However, in order for education to be truly engaging and effective, students need to see a deeper connection between what they are learning and their own lives. Many school districts have attempted to do this by creating magnet schools and academies based on student interests. Many of these have been highly successful, but they do not meet the needs of the majority of students.

Instead, a system needs to be devised that involves as many students as possible in high-interest activities that result in real learning. These activities need to be interdisciplinary and provide students with many different paths to success. By tying learning to real life, students are more likely to be engaged and successful.

ESSENTIAL

Learning communities are a way that some high schools have attempted to make education more relevant for all students. For example, a school might create a couple of learning communities within their school, and have each focus on different topics. Students get to choose to work within the community that interests them most.

A New Way to Look at Curriculum

One method of achieving these aims is through interdisciplinary projects. For example, teachers collaborate to create a project that presents students with a problem, such as the need to build a new bridge. However, in order for this to occur, the voters need to pass a referendum agreeing to pay extra taxes. An architectural committee needs to investigate the history and art of bridges to make recommendations and create drawings and models. An environmental impact statement needs to be created that examines the effects of construction on the environment. The actual design of the bridge requires the integration of mathematics and science. Obviously, the teachers would help guide each of these actions with individual lessons and materials. The teachers would work together to assess each part of the project as it was completed.

It may be asked how each teacher grades a project such as this. One possibility would be that instead of expecting to pass each of the "standards" for a course sequentially or within the same year, students could pass standards individually and progress through each course at their own pace.

The idea of project-based instruction has been around for a long time. However, it is very hard for a teacher to implement this methodology. Trying to create an interdisciplinary project is even harder in the current educational system.

Obviously, the system described above would not work the way things stand today in education. A new approach to education, standards, and student learning is required.

Twenty-first Century Skills

Twenty-first century skills are common educational buzzwords used in discussions of changes in education. Different organizations define these in slightly different ways, but they all focus on the new skills that students need to thrive in today's world. The Partnership for 21st Century Skills based in Tucson, Arizona is a group that was developed to help advance these skills. This organization began in 2002 as a partnership between the U.S. Department of Education, co-founders Ken Kay and Diny Golder-Dardis, and the following groups:

- AOL Time Warner Foundation
- Apple Computer, Inc.
- Cable in the Classroom
- Cisco Systems, Inc.
- Dell Computer Corporation
- Microsoft Computer Corporation
- National Education Association
- SAP

According to their website, the mission of the Partnership for 21st Century Skills is to "Serve as a catalyst to position twenty-first century skills at the center of U.S. K–12 education by building collaborative partnerships among education, business, community and government leaders." The Partnership believes that a gap exists between what is being taught in schools and what students really need to know to thrive in the twenty-first century.

Educational leaders are often at odds concerning the focus of education. One major debate concerns skills-based education versus a focus on content. Some argue that focusing on skills causes content to fall by the wayside. However, Ken Kay has stated, "There's no question from the beginning that our work has been built on the premise that skills and content support each other, and the notion that you have to choose between them is a false dichotomy."

What the Student Should Learn

The Partnership for 21st Century Skills focuses on two aspects of an effective education: student outcomes and support systems. The first of these, student outcomes, deals with what students need to learn in order to succeed in the twenty-first century. Students should still learn the core subjects; however, these should be informed with specific themes to help elevate student learning, including:

- Global awareness
- Financial, economic, business, and entrepreneurial literacy
- Civic literacy
- Health literacy

Further, as students work to learn the core subjects, they also need to master learning and innovation skills, information, media and technology skills, and life and career skills. By deliberately integrating these skills and themes into the core curriculum, students will be able to make connections and become adept problem solvers.

Twenty-first Century Learning Environment

A necessary part to achieving the Partnership's stated goals is the creation of the 21st Century Support System. In order for teachers to be successful implementing the necessary changes and teaching the skills and themes listed above, the Partnership has developed many tools to help them along the way. Support and guidance is given in the following areas:

- Standards
- Assessments
- Curriculum and instruction
- Professional development
- Learning environments

By working through each of these areas, the Partnership for 21st Century Skills hopes to help students become more adept and meet the challenges of a competitive global market.

Taking Learning to a Higher Level

Today, researchers and educational experts across the United States are working to come up with solutions for what many perceive as an educational crisis. Some of this research is focused on the way that students learn, while other studies are looking at the way teachers present their information. All of this is very exciting to the new and veteran teacher, as it provides new avenues for reaching and engaging all students. However, it can also be scary. The task of changing our teaching methods can seem daunting and we would need to adjust what we think about education. We, as educators, as well as our colleges of education must be willing to adapt as new information arises.

FACT

The brain is made up of many neurons that are able to transmit information to each other over long distances through their axons. While the number of neurons that a person has is pretty much set at birth, except for a couple of areas of the brain, the connections between axons continue to develop as a child grows.

Brain Research

Each year new achievements are made in our understanding of the human brain. This research can be used to great effect by parents and educators alike. For example, some of the latest research has shown that the brain can perceive parts and the whole at the same time. This indicates that it is important for educators to make sure they continually make connections between facts and the overall context of the information they are teaching. Other research shows that emotions and learning cannot be separated. Therefore, if students are upset, tense, or negative about their own abilities, they will not be able to learn as easily. Build a positive classroom experience for students to help them have a safe place where they can learn.

A Different Way to Approach Students

It is easy for teachers to fall into the mindset that students are required to attend school and must do whatever is asked to earn good grades. There is no real room for the student's desires in the equation. However, one group, the Schlechty Center, believes that this notion should be challenged. As they say on their website, schools should move away from being "organizations based on the assumption that the core business of schools has to do with producing compliance and attendance to organizations where the core business focuses on nurturing attention and commitment." All teachers know that while they can in some ways "force" students to attend their classes, they cannot make students learn the material. The teachers' focus is in their control.

ALERT

If your school district provides training and supports a new method for approaching students and teaching, then you will need to learn and use this method. However, if your district does not do this, then you are free to learn as much as you can about each and pick and choose the best to implement in your classroom.

The Schlechty Center is a group focused on bringing about true school reform. One of the foundations of their method is called the "Working on the Work" program. The purpose of this program is to help educators focus on what makes schoolwork truly engaging for students. According to founder Phil Schlechty, there are at least ten qualities that can make schoolwork more engaging for students, including items such as choice, novelty, and variety. By learning to incorporate these qualities, teachers can appeal to their students and make them more apt to learn and achieve.

Building a New Mindset

In order to take education to the next level, teachers need to be the catalyst for change. Sometimes this can be very challenging, especially when you are teaching at a school that does not have either the money or the inclination to pay for programs such as those described here. But this does not mean that you should just throw up your hands and resign yourself to teach the way teachers always have.

Fortunately, teachers have many excellent resources available at the click of a mouse. Information about the programs and research described here can all be accessed through the Internet. Even if you can't afford to go through a specific program, by looking through each of these websites you can gain ideas that can be implemented immediately in your classroom. For example, the Schlechty Center has published on the web the ten qualities of engaging instruction mentioned above. Just by ensuring that at least one of those qualities is in every lesson you present to your students, you have already begun increasing your own effectiveness as a teacher.

CHAPTER 22

Online Learning: The Wave of the Future

With the advent of the Internet, teaching and learning has moved beyond the walls of the traditional classroom. Students and parents today have an increasing amount of control over education. With the rise of quality institutions, online learning may prove to be a big part of the solution to many of education's ills. The future looks bright for this exciting new area of education.

What Is Online Education?

Online education can take many forms. It can range from the traditional idea of distance learning to something much more teacher driven. This chapter will focus on the teacher-driven model, using the Florida Virtual School as an example.

In this context, students receive instructional materials and turn in assignments through the Internet. However, they have a teacher for each course who stays in close contact through phone calls, discussions boards, online chats, and e-mail messages. Students are able to work whenever they want—even if it is 3 A.M. Teachers also have the flexibility to set their own hours during the day, since they too work from home.

State of Online Education Today

Online or virtual education is only about fifteen years old, and each year numerous online schools emerge as educators and politicians realize the potential of online learning. One of the constants of online education today is change. Because technology changes so rapidly, the state of online education is continuously in flux. One thing is certain: Online learning is here to stay.

QUESTION

How many students are enrolled in virtual school classes?
The forty virtual schools studied by the Peak Group reported a combined enrollment of 85,500 students in 2001–2002. However, this number continues to grow significantly each year and is estimated to be between 700,000 and 800,000 in 2009.

Online Programs

Because it is so new, little research exists to measure the effectiveness of online education. Part of the problem is the wide variety of programs that make it hard to define and collect information. Just as with traditional schools, there are excellent programs as well as programs that are almost certainly doomed to fail.

In 2002, the Peak Group completed a study that recognized forty schools across the nation as leaders in online learning. Of these, fifteen schools provide the entire curriculum for the courses offered. The other twenty-five provide supplements to traditional classroom learning.

Online teaching opportunities are available for teachers with vision. Each year the number of teaching opportunities grows. Some schools have part-time opportunities for educators who wish to become involved in this exciting form of teaching. While teaching online is not for everyone, it does provide many benefits and can be a rewarding career.

Case Study: The Florida Virtual School

The Florida Virtual School (FLVS) is a leader in online education. The school was awarded the Excellence in Distance Learning Programming, Pre-K–12 Education award in 2000, 2002, and 2003 by the United States Distance Learning Association. It was further awarded the USDLA Twenty-first Century Awards Best Practices in Distance Learning Award in 2005 and 2007. This accredited program provides a wide range of courses for elementary, middle, and high school students.

When students sign up for courses, they are also assigned a teacher who helps them throughout the course. In fact, the hands-on role of the teacher makes FLVS effective. Teachers place monthly phone calls, create monthly progress reports, and are always available to answer questions through e-mail and over the phone.

The Florida Virtual School prides itself on the level of parental involvement in each student's education. By talking each month to both the students and their parents, educators gain partners whose sole goal is to help their child succeed. This is something that sets FLVS apart from other education providers.

The motto of FLVS is, "Any time, any place, any path, any pace." This means that students have a variety of choices to help them take control of their education. Further, teachers work hard with students to create individualized learning programs. While students do have deadlines to meet as they complete courses, they also have a huge amount of flexibility that is not afforded them in traditional schools.

The Wave of the Future

Online teaching will continue to become more important in solving some of the major problems of education. This type of education is not for every learner or teacher. However, it provides another choice that can help relieve some of the inequalities in education. While it is not likely that online education will ever completely replace the traditional classroom, quality education over the Internet will continue to grow and develop until it is a viable alternative for all students.

ESSENTIAL

While online learning is the wave of the future, it is not equally available to all students. Some schools and districts feel threatened by online schools because they see them taking funding and teachers. As a result, schools actually discourage their students from taking online courses.

Crowded Schools and Teacher Shortages

School crowding is a nationwide epidemic. Many school districts do not have the money to keep up with growing populations of students and just cannot afford to build enough schools. Consequently, schools become overcrowded. Some turn to solutions like double sessions—half the student body goes to school in the morning and half in the afternoon—but this situation is not in anyone's best interest.

Combine overcrowding with a shortage of qualified teachers, and you have a problem of epic proportions. Online education can truly help this situation. By having students complete work at home or in a school computer lab, more students can be accommodated with fewer resources. If a school sets up a lab and uses online courses, they can hire a lab facilitator who does not have to have a teaching degree and does not get paid a teacher's salary.

A Lack of Choices

While many schools provide students with a wide range of curriculum choices, others offer little more than the core curriculum. Many rural schools are actually "undercrowded" and experience teacher shortages.

These schools find it difficult to offer a broad range of classes and may not have any Advanced Placement courses at all. Online education can help fill in the gaps.

ALERT

Unfortunately, because of the cost of technology and the state of Internet connections in rural communities, some students have a difficult time using online programs. Many states are extending grants and funding opportunities to students and areas to help them get the access that will enhance their education.

One student in an AP U.S. History course with FLVS wrote, "I live in such a small rural town that there are no AP classes of any sort offered in my high school, and FLVS has been a lifesaver. Thanks for giving me the opportunity to take a class I never would have had in high school!" The opportunities provided to this student were unavailable through his local school system. Such students who feel left behind because of their school's limits now find themselves on a level playing field when competing with other students for college admission and scholarships.

Special Education Students

Many students who have learning disabilities find that online education affords them greater flexibility for completion and achievement. Because students can work when they choose, they have the ability to take their time learning lessons. In a classroom setting, a teacher might present information for fifty minutes, leaving some students behind; students online control how long it takes them to go through a lesson. Many online schools, such as FLVS, also have an instructor ready and willing to help students understand any areas where they are having difficulties. The flexibility, extra time, and help can truly make the difference for these students.

Courses at FLVS are compatible with computer programs that assist students with disabilities. For example, "readers" are programs that orally present the material on the Internet to students with visual impairments. The course material from FLVS is written in a logical manner specifically for these programs.

Unique Situations

Online learning has had a huge impact on those students unable to attend a traditional school. For example, sick and homebound students are able to take courses without leaving their homes. Students who have psychological problems, for example, those with agoraphobia (a fear of crowds), can still learn the curriculum while building relationships with others in a safe, online environment.

Students who are excellent athletes or who are working as actors, actresses, or entertainers and who are not home very often find online learning to be a wonderful alternative to tutors. These students can log on from wherever they are traveling and complete their work. They can participate in discussions with their instructors and other students to help them feel connected to a school even when they do not have one in the traditional sense. Further, their curriculum is standardized so they receive the same education as their peers in a traditional school setting.

Online Learning and Homeschooling

One final area in which online learning has made a huge impact is homeschooling. Parents choose to homeschool their students for many reasons. Some parents do so for religious reasons, while others do not want students exposed to dangerous behaviors in their traditional local school. By providing homeschooled students with curriculum based on state and national standards, educators ensure that students receive a quality education even if they are not enrolled in traditional school.

The Mind of an Online Instructor

The mind of an online instructor works completely differently from a traditional teacher's. For one thing, the online instructor has to be much more flexible. Whereas in a traditional classroom all students are basically in the same place at the same time, in the online environment students are all over the board. One student might be working in an early unit, while another is just about done with her coursework. This situation does take some getting used to, but it is better for students because it does not force them all to conform to the same schedule.

Online teaching is much more individualized. Students and teachers get to know each other very well through phone calls. While most online schools have schedules that students have to follow in order to keep moving through the courses, there is much more room for flexibility. If students start the year late, they are not considered behind. They do not have to "make up" work and "catch up" with the other students. They start on an individualized schedule and follow it the same way as other students in a formal school would. In other words, the schedule is fitted to the student, not the student to the schedule.

ALERT

There is a steep learning curve for teaching online. It typically takes about three years for a teacher to truly feel comfortable in the online environment. This is due to the many differences in attitude, delivery methods, and teaching practices between the traditional and virtual settings.

Benefits of Teaching Online

Online instructors have many benefits. Imagine never having to deal with tardy students, absences, disruptions, school violence, fire drills, or even getting up in the morning and driving to work. These benefits are huge and cannot be overestimated. But precisely because it allows for so much freedom, online teaching requires a lot of self-discipline.

Another surprising benefit of online instruction is that it allows you to really get to know your students, sometimes even better than in the traditional classroom. This is because a traditional class might consist of thirty students that a teacher sees for only fifty minutes each day. It is impossible to truly connect with each and every student—there is just not enough time. However, online learning provides one-on-one learning opportunities as teachers call and talk to their students. There is an opportunity to get to know them as people and not just as pupils in a classroom.

Parents can also become much more involved in their kids' education through an online learning environment. Many online schools provide parents with access to their children's work and send them monthly progress reports. Teachers are usually required to call and talk to parents at least once a month. Many traditional-school parents never hear from their students' teachers the entire year!

Issues for Online Instructors

Just as there are many benefits to online teaching and learning, teachers need to be aware of and deal with certain issues. As stated previously, some teachers will be happier teaching in the traditional classroom than in the online environment. However, if these issues can be overcome, then online teaching can be a truly rewarding experience.

A Different Environment

Teaching from your home can be a very different experience than teaching in a classroom. For one thing, you have to show a great sense of self-control so that you actually sit down each day and do your work. Further, you will not be interacting with "live" people each day—instead, you'll be working online or talking on the phone. Many people have a hard time adjusting to this and miss the human interactions of a traditional school.

It is much harder to separate work life from home life when you work at home. Work can easily consume an inordinate amount of time, thereby leading to family issues and problems. While you can leave the traditional classroom at the end of the day, your work is always with you at home. Students are constantly e-mailing and turning in work. Knowing when to turn off the computer takes just as much self-discipline as knowing when to turn it on.

Finally, just as in traditional schools, you will be asked from time to time to perform extra duties. It is important to keep in mind that many of these extra duties will probably be completed during your own time. This means that your work schedule can quickly eat into your "life schedule." If you keep your priorities straight, you will be a much happier person and employee.

Time Commitment

Online learning does require a huge time commitment from the teacher, in a different way than in the traditional classroom. While online teachers do not necessarily work more hours than traditional teachers, they do have a very different schedule. This can make them feel like they are working more than in the regular classroom. This is partly because students can work any time and can ask questions any time. Therefore, you will probably need to check e-mail and voice messages every day of the week, including weekends.

Further, the students who go to traditional school will not be available for phone calls and other communication during normal working hours. Therefore, you will be making many phone calls in the evenings and on weekends. Online teaching requires flexibility.

Be Wary of Cheating

One final concern of many online teachers is cheating. Just as in the traditional classroom, online cheating does occur. Because teachers are not seeing their students complete their exams or work in class, it is difficult to be assured that the work turned in is truly their own. That is where phone calls come into play. Online teachers must use phone calls to verify the knowledge of their students.

Online instructors also have the tools of the Internet at their disposal to help determine whether something has been plagiarized. If you think that a student has directly copied something, you can copy and paste the sentence into a search engine and see if any direct matches come up. Of course, this will not help for work that has been copied from written texts, but it does help control plagiarism issues.

Tips for Success in Online Teaching

In the end, success in online teaching is no different than success in the traditional classroom. Teachers must make policies that they stick to and create a positive, warm learning environment. Although teachers do not see their students in person, they still can convey their high expectations through comments and phone calls. An important benefit of online learning is that teachers can truly work to meet the needs of each individual student in a way that they could not in the traditional classroom.

Phone Calls

Phone calls are probably the most important factor in having a successful career as an online instructor. When teachers do not call their students each month, they find that some students actually work less or stop working altogether. Students will feel disconnected and parents will not be a central part of their child's education.

ALERT

Online educators spend a great deal of time trying to reach students who are not home. Set up times for students to contact you, or have students send you windows of time when they will be available. This will cut down on the time you spend making phone calls.

While the time it takes to make phone calls can sometimes be daunting, by dividing the phone calls into small daily amounts, you will be able to achieve your goals of reaching each student. Some phone calls will require more time if, for instance, a student is struggling or not working. Take this into consideration when setting aside time for those calls. Also, it would be a very good idea to schedule more than one phone call a month with those students.

Staying Flexible

Just as with the traditional classroom, an essential quality of an effective teacher is flexibility. Even more than in the traditional classroom, online teachers have to accept and embrace change and uncertainty. They have to be willing to have students starting at different times during the year. They also have to understand that the Internet is a continually changing environment, and they might have to adjust to new teaching platforms every couple of years. Only flexible individuals will be able to thrive and be happy in an online teaching environment. They will also find great rewards for being involved in such an exciting endeavor.

CHAPTER 23

Dealing with the Unexpected

It is the first day of planning week before school actually begins. You are excited and ready to change some lives. Then you receive your class assignments. You have five different courses to teach. On top of this, you will not even have a room of your own! All the excitement you felt when you got up this morning is gone. You are feeling overwhelmed and scared. What can you do? Hopefully, this chapter will provide you with some ideas to help deal with these and other possible situations that might arise.

Expect the Unexpected

Your first order of business as a teacher is to expect the unexpected. Realize that things will probably not go as you planned. The situation described in the opening of this chapter may not be typical, but it can and does occur. If it seems really scary to you, realize that you can still follow the principles of being an effective teacher and end up having a good year.

Your reaction and success depend on your attitude and the way you face each new situation. Actively look for ways to improve your situation at every turn. Do not just assume there is nothing you can do. Instead, work with what you do have to create a good experience for yourself and your students. If you do not believe that you can work under the conditions set before you, then you will be right. Similarly, if you believe that you can make it through the year, you will be right too.

Not Enough Texts

The fact is that textbooks cost a lot of money. Unfortunately, many school districts are facing budget crunches, and textbooks are often where schools and districts cut costs. You may find that when you go into your classroom on the first day, you have fewer books than you have students. You will not be able to send books home with students, which means that you will not be able to assign readings from the book to be completed at home. If you are lucky, you will have enough books to create a class set. If you are not so lucky, you will not have any textbooks at all.

Class Sets

Class sets of textbooks are common in classrooms across the United States. As previously stated, textbooks are very expensive. If one textbook costs a school fifty dollars, you can see that purchasing 300 texts (enough for two teachers with full loads) would be very expensive. Many school districts that have money shortages may choose to spend less on texts. They often figure that if each teacher has at least one set for the class to share, they will be able to continue using the texts for their curriculum. Rarely does a school purchase texts for more than a few classes in any given year.

However, record keeping and organization can pose real problems for teachers using class sets. Teachers have to devise systems for keeping track of their books at all times. If a student has been sick, teachers have to arrange for them to check out a text for the evening to make up work. Unfortunately, if a teacher has exactly the number of texts he needs for his classes, he may not even be able to let a student take a book for the evening. (Ideas and systems of organization for dealing with textbooks are reviewed in Chapter 7.)

FACT

Textbook costs have risen in the United States at a faster rate than in other countries. The number of textbooks available for any one subject is limited, so competition does not have a great effect on price. Because of necessity, the demand for texts does not lessen dramatically with increased prices.

No Texts

Worse than having to use class sets is the situation where you have no textbooks at all. While this will most likely happen because of budget constraints, there are some schools that frown on textbook use completely. Some administrators feel that texts lend themselves to a lecture and busywork mentality. By removing textbooks, they hope that teachers will turn to other more creative methods of content delivery.

This situation can be really hard for the new teacher. It is one thing for a teacher who has many years' experience teaching a course to be told she will no longer have a textbook. It is another for a novice to be presented with this situation.

Veteran teachers have probably collected great lesson ideas and supporting information over the years to supplement the text. With a little extra effort, they may be able to do a fine job presenting the material without a text. However, novice teachers do not have this experience. They do not have the time or energy to create their own curriculum in the beginning. In most cases, they are still trying to figure out how to best deal with student disruptions and organization issues.

If you are placed in this situation, find yourself a good textbook or set of books to use as your guide even if you do not use it with your students. Try to get your school to purchase supporting material and ready-made lessons to help you get through the year. Keep your eye out for anything that you might find useful. Lesson ideas can come from unexpected places. If you have real concerns about your lack of texts, talk to your mentor or other veteran teachers. Many times, teachers will have old lessons and worksheets that you can adapt for your classroom situation.

ESSENTIAL

Many texts are accompanied by support material that can be adapted for use. Even if you are unable to use a text, you may still be able to use some of the accompanying materials. Also, do not underestimate the ideas in the teacher's edition of textbooks.

Outdated and Inaccurate Texts

Sometimes the textbooks you have to use are so old that the information is inaccurate or obsolete. For example, if your school has not replaced its geography books since the breakup of the Soviet Union, you cannot effectively teach about that part of the world using that book. Therefore, you will need to supplement this information with material from magazines, news sites, and other books to give your students the correct information. Unfortunately, this can mean extra work for you. When you do need to supplement a text because it is outdated, keep your lessons simple.

Textbooks are written by humans, who can make mistakes. Textbook writers and editors also have personal biases that make it into texts. Furthermore, interest groups and influential states can have a huge impact on what is and what is not included in a text. All of this means that you need to read the text critically before you create assignments for students. This ensures that you are not reinforcing inaccurate or biased information. As you move through your teaching career, you may wish to have students examine certain pages or chapters in their texts for inaccuracies or bias as an interesting assignment.

Overcrowded Classes

Overcrowding at schools is almost a given in most areas of the country. Even though the school you work for might publish a fairly good teacher-to-student ratio, this number is usually inaccurate in terms of what really happens in the classrooms around campus. There are many teachers who have very small or no classes. For example, there might be a special education co-teacher who is in classes all day long with another teacher. This counts as two teachers in the room and therefore reduces the overall number of students for each teacher in the school.

ALERT

By counting nontraditional teachers with few students in their classes in a student-to-teacher ratio, districts may feel justified in hiring fewer classroom teachers. The ratio does not reflect reality, however. What is listed as a 27:1 ratio might actually be 33:1. Therefore, little relief is provided for overcrowded classes.

Even worse, some schools count people who would not traditionally be thought of as teachers. For example, if a guidance counselor also has a few student aides, the counselor might be counted as a teacher for the purposes of the ratio. This is not to say that counselors are not teaching their student aides important skills. However, it does give an inaccurate picture of school loads.

Discipline Issues

If you are faced with thirty-five or forty kids in a class, you will find that many problems are magnified by overcrowding. What would be minor discipline issues in smaller classrooms can quickly escalate in crowded classes.

More than in any other situation, you need to have a firm hand when it comes to discipline in an overcrowded classroom. You cannot allow this type of class to get out of control, because getting them back on task can be nearly impossible. Make sure that you strictly follow your discipline plan as you teach each day.

Changes to Lessons

Large classes make interesting assignments like debates and simulations more challenging. Therefore, think about the logistics of an activity before you put it in your lesson plan. Place careful limits on each of the types of activities you attempt.

Further, you will want to make clear rules concerning class discussions. Many teachers become lax when it comes to making students raise their hands to make comments. However, with a large group, it is imperative that you have students raise their hands to be recognized simply to keep order.

Finally, realize that you have to grade whatever you assign. The difference between grading twenty and forty essays can be huge. This does not mean that you should shirk your teaching duties to lessen your workload. However, it does mean that you should try to avoid giving two grading-intensive assignments right after each other. Plan to give yourself a break every once in a while.

Not Enough Desks

Overcrowded classrooms lead to a shortage of desks for students. As previously discussed, you should not make students feel uncomfortable for being in your classroom. Realize that the desk situation is a temporary one. For one thing, classes are often unbalanced during the first week or two of school, so you may lose some of the students to another class. Further, you may find that the teachers around you have smaller classes than you do, in which case they'll give you some of their desks.

If a couple of days of the school year have passed and students are still sitting on the floor of your classroom, talk with your administrator. Remember, these kids will tell their parents, who will probably call and complain to the school about the situation. Even though you did not cause the situation, you might find that the parents blame you. Therefore, be proactive and make sure that the office knows of your predicament. They will work out a solution.

No Classroom at All

Being a "floater" is one of the worst situations a new teacher can be placed in. This means that you do not have a permanent classroom, but move into classrooms when other teachers have planning periods. In other words, first period might mean you are in Mrs. Smith's classroom because she has planning first period. Second period might mean you move to Mr. Jones's classroom because he has planning at that time. And you keep moving from classroom to classroom throughout the day. Obviously, this is not conducive to helping you feel comfortable your first year, and it can pose some real challenges. Yet, if you can face the challenges of "floating," you will be that much closer to becoming a truly effective teacher.

Organizing Yourself

One of the first keys to success is to create a system of organization. Typically, a school will provide a "floating" teacher with a cart. Create sections in your cart and permanent places for important information. For example, keep your lesson plan book and your attendance papers in the same spot every day so you can easily access them.

Because you are moving from class to class and you have little if any time to catch your breath, you will find that staying organized can be a real challenge. Since you will probably be packing up your items after the dismissal bell rings, you will have little time to use a complicated organizational system. Go for simplicity.

You should purchase a portable file box to take with you from class to class. This allows you to keep student work and your papers organized and private. Remember that it is your obligation to protect the privacy of your students' work.

Planning Periods

A teacher's planning period is a truly important part of her day. For one thing, it is typically a time to come off the "stage" of teaching and take a silent break. It can be a peaceful, regenerative experience if treated correctly. However, as a "floater" it can be difficult to find a peaceful place to do your planning, grade your students' papers, or even just to catch your breath. Some schools make sure to provide teachers with the space to work before and after school and during planning. However, some schools leave "floaters" to find room for themselves. It is important that you spend some time finding this personal space and that you treat it as such.

Issues with Other Teachers

One of the biggest problems for "floaters" is interacting with other teachers. Since you are using someone else's room, you will face many issues not encountered by teachers with assigned classrooms. Many teachers feel that their room is their personal space, and by entering it—even reluctantly—you are violating their space. You make them move for their planning so they cannot even work at their desks. You sit at their desks. In other words, you are an intruder.

ALERT

To avoid problems with teachers while you are "floating," spend the last two to three minutes of each period straightening up the classroom and picking up trash. Many teachers who are unhappy sharing their room will focus on the condition in which you leave it each day.

It's possible you will find some hostility on the part of teachers whose classrooms you will need to borrow, especially if they are veterans. Some teachers may even be downright rude to you. Through it all, make sure that you treat each room you enter as your own. This means that you give some thought to picking up and taking care of everything in the room. In the end, remember that no teacher "owns" a classroom. They are assigned a room by the administration. If the principal wanted to, he could change all room assignments each year. Even though you should continue to be thoughtful, do not become a doormat because of other teachers' issues.

Multiple Preps

Teaching more than one subject in a term is known as having multiple preps. For example, you might be assigned to teach regular biology and advanced/honors biology. This requires two different lesson plans. The worst situation, however, is to have four or more preps. If you have that many classes to create curriculum for, you can quickly become overwhelmed.

Organization Is Key

Again, it is very important to stay organized. One good idea is to use colored folders for each class. That way, you can tell without looking at the title of a file which class it is associated with. As soon as a piece of paper crosses your desk, categorize it and stick it in the correct folder.

Ask for Help

It should not embarrass you to ask for help. In fact, when all is said and done, those who do not ask but act anyway are the ones who appear to be foolish. Asking for help can be as simple as discussing your problems with other teachers over lunch. Self-reliance is a great thing. However, those who truly make it do so by "standing on the shoulders of giants." If you happen to have multiple preps *and* float, realize that the ability to adapt is within you.

Do Not Reinvent the Wheel

A year in which you are given multiple preps is not the year to try all kinds of new things. Do not create complicated lesson plans for yourself. Keep things simple so that you can actually have a life outside of school. Realize that you will probably not be the most creative teacher you can be because of your situation. However, you are learning important skills to help you in all classes and the future.

In Case of Emergency

Most of your teaching days will be fairly normal. You might have a few disruptions occur each day, but there will not be many incidents that completely stop education in your classroom or the school for extended periods of time. This is a blessing because major disruptions or emergencies can take a great deal of recovery time. Students often find it quite difficult to focus on mundane schoolwork after a three-hour jaunt to the stadium because of a bomb threat.

However, large disruptions will occur. They can range from the harmless to the severe, and can include the following:

- Surprise fire and tornado drills
- Actual fires and tornadoes
- Bomb threats and scares
- Classroom and school-wide power outages
- Incidents of school violence
- Tragic loss of a student or teacher
- Tragic world events that affect the students
- School pranks and vandalism

This list is not meant to scare you. However, it is good to be aware of situations that might occur and to have an idea of how you should react. Most schools have established plans to deal with many of these issues. Make sure you have your attendance and grade book readily available because it will be a necessity during emergencies.

As a new teacher, you can look at the unexpected as a scary proposition or as a challenge waiting to be met. Your attitude will carry over into your day-to-day teaching. More importantly, it will influence your students in ways you cannot even imagine.

CHAPTER 24

Survival Mode:
First Day, First Week

While you will spend a lot of time getting ready for the first day, nothing can match the actual experience of it. As a new teacher, you can expect to spend more time just trying to survive than doing anything else. You will devote many hours trying to keep yourself organized and dealing with new situations as they occur. The best way to not only survive but also thrive from the very beginning is to be as prepared as possible.

The Right Learning Environment

The effectiveness of your learning environment depends on you. If you create a roomful of distractions, you will probably have a lot of distracted students. However, if you create an atmosphere where learning is expected and rewarded, many students will actually learn in your classroom.

Organization Breeds Confidence

One of the biggest problems for new teachers is dealing with all the paperwork and minutiae of teaching. Many times, new teachers enter the classroom not realizing that they need systems for dealing with late work, tardies, absences, and taking attendance. Without a system of organization in your room, much time will be wasted dealing with mundane, housekeeping issues.

ESSENTIAL

Once you have your initial organizational system in place, you should spend five to ten minutes each day straightening your desk and room. If you allow papers to build up without putting them where they need to go, you will end up in a state of disorganization very quickly.

Using the advice given in this book, create your own system of organization for each of these issues. Decide before the first day how you are going to distribute make-up work. Decide what you are going to do about late work. Waiting until a situation arises to deal with it will probably result in lost time and energy, so spend some time up front to get organized, and you will be able to save much time later.

Remember that organizing does not stop with your room and your belongings. You should also have a well-thought-out discipline plan in place and ready to go. Students will try you during the first week of school. If you have a system in place, you will feel more confident as you deal with disruptions and other unexpected situations.

The Value of Education

As you may have noticed, one of the main themes throughout this book is the value of creating high expectations both for yourself and for your students. Of course, your expectations must be based on reality. But they must also be based on the idea that education is important and valuable. Believe it or not, there are teachers who do not see the value in education. Needless to say, students learn very little in their classes.

Education is important for so many reasons. It broadens horizons, making students more willing to be accepting and understanding. It gives students a sense of the past, allowing them to go forward with a basis for making decisions. It teaches students skills that will help them succeed in their lives after school. However, the ultimate goal of education should be to instill a desire to learn. Students should leave school armed with the tools to be able to continue their education on their own.

FACT

Education can bring tangible rewards. According to the Employment Policy Foundation, the average individual who earns a bachelor's degree can expect to earn nearly double that of a high school graduate over her lifetime.

Realize that there is so much information available that no one can ever "know it all." In fact, you can expect your students to forget between 50 and 75 percent or more of what they learn in your class as soon as they leave it. This leads some people to argue that teaching individual facts and having students memorize things is a waste of their time and yours.

However, unless an individual knows some basic information, he will appear ignorant. Basic facts are also necessary in the scaffolding of new information. People learn new information and remember it for the long term by connecting it to already existing information in long-term memory. If there is a weakness in a child's educational past, it will become magnified as he progresses through school. It is a false belief that memorization holds no place in education, although, education should be much more than just memorizing lists of terms and concepts.

Attitude Is Everything

You must enter your first week of school with a positive attitude and the desire to succeed. That first week can be very scary and nerve-wracking at times. However, realize that in just a few weeks you will have figured out much of the everyday tasks and will be able to truly focus on teaching effective lessons.

Staying Positive

Positive people are ones who succeed. They do not necessarily believe that everything is rosy, but they do believe that even if bad things happen, in the end everything will work out okay. Have this attitude as you teach, and you will be well rewarded. When you feel that things are going pretty badly, it may help to remind yourself that this, too, will pass. You basically have two choices in life: let events "happen" to you, or actively participate in each event in your life. Positive people are proactive; they strive to make the best of every situation.

Clear Expectations

Start the year off right by letting students know your expectations for yourself and for them. Tell your students that you know that they can learn and you expect them to put forth their best effort. Further, help them understand what they should expect from you.

A common theme throughout this book has been that your expectations are truly essential. They are important for student success and your own career as an educator. Do not underestimate the power of high positive expectations.

Remember, there is a difference between being in power and being respected. As a teacher, you are in a position of power; however, this does not automatically mean you will be respected. Only by acting consistently and fairly will students begin to respect you.

Enjoying Interaction with Students

It is amazing that some teachers do not like young people. These teachers typically love their subjects, but they consider students to be a necessary annoyance factor that comes along with the job. Thankfully, not many people like this stay in the teaching profession for long.

You will spend the majority of your time with your students. It is essential that you like them and, more importantly, like the people you hope they will become. The education profession is all about being positive. If you cannot look for the good in your students, then you should not be teaching.

You will find that in your local community there is a perception that kids today are worse than in the past. This is a mistake; kids today are no better and no worse than they were yesterday. However, the few truly disruptive students are the ones who garner all the press.

Youth culture may be different and sometimes hard to understand, but if you look back to when you were a child, you may have heard adults questioning the values of your peer group. The generation gap is a known phenomenon that spans history. Because students are just children looking to find their own way in life, their attitudes, likes, and dislikes may seem foreign to you. Just because something is different does not automatically make it bad.

Dealing with Nervousness

You will most probably experience some nervousness before and during your first day of school. It may be the fear of the unknown, or the result of the excitement of beginning a new endeavor. There are two ways of dealing with nervousness. You can choose to dwell on it, or you can work through it and focus on the excitement of beginning a new challenge.

Look Beyond Yourself

One way to fight nervousness is to take the focus away from yourself and place it on others instead. Realize that your students are probably nervous too. By focusing on them and trying to make them feel more at ease, you will ease your own fears at the same time. Practice active listening techniques starting from the first day, and try to get to know a few students at a time in the moments before and after class. Just having a friendly face in the room can be a huge lifesaver.

Fake It

Your students have expectations from the moment they walk into your classroom. They expect you to be in charge of the class. One way to fight nervousness is just to fake it. You can feel completely nervous on the inside, but on the outside exude calm. If your students feel that you are nervous, they might try to take advantage of the situation. You could lose control of things from the beginning.

Do not broadcast to your students that you are a new teacher. Emphasize your previous teaching experience, even if it was just as an intern. By highlighting your teaching experience, you will be letting your students know that you are not an easy target. Students will look to your attitude about things and situations. If you overreact on the first day, this will be seen as a weakness and a sign of inexperience. If you take things in stride and show a sense of humor while remaining firm, you can have a successful class and quickly calm the butterflies in your stomach.

Before the Students Arrive

You will most likely have a few days or a week of planning before the students actually arrive. Some of this time will be spent in meetings. However, much of this time will be spent alone in your room. Sometimes it can be overwhelming to think about all of the preparations you need to finish before students arrive. Spend some time creating a checklist of everything you wish to accomplish. Realize that it is much easier to get things done before the students arrive on their first day of class than after classes begin.

ESSENTIAL

Planning week will seem to fly by. It is important that you network and meet your fellow educators during this time. However, you need to make sure that you are not spending too much time socializing instead of preparing yourself and your room.

You should also spend a portion of your planning week getting to know the school staff and the teachers around you. Introduce yourself and let the teachers around you know that you are new to the school. Ask them for advice. Many times, teachers will share information that you will not receive from administration or others. Further, by building these relationships from the beginning, you can have people to turn to when problems arise.

The First Day

The first day of school will most probably go by very quickly. You will be performing some standard housekeeping tasks and dealing with students with scheduling problems entering and leaving your class at different times. Even though you will not get a lot done in terms of curriculum on that first day, you have the opportunity to set the stage for the rest of the year.

Begin Immediately

Begin your course on the first day. Try to finish your housekeeping duties quickly, leaving five or ten minutes to start your course. Have a mini-lesson planned or give a pretest. Hold a class discussion about expectations concerning your course. Discuss a current event that has a bearing on what your students will be learning. In other words, send kids the message that even though it might just be the first day, you mean business.

ALERT

If you choose to begin work on the first day of class, expect your students to complain. Many teachers will bend to these complaints. However, if you really want to reinforce your ideas about work and expectations, you should simply ignore the complaints and continue with your lesson.

If you talk to students, you will find that they have teachers who make them work and teachers who allow them to goof off. These labels are placed on teachers from the first day. Worse still, they follow you from year to year. It is very hard—though not impossible—to change your reputation. It is an uphill battle to suddenly become a teacher who requires hard work when you have been lax in the past.

Learning Students' Names

Learning names can sometimes be a difficult prospect for new teachers. However, if you know your students' names, you have a better chance of connecting with them and also controlling their behavior. A great technique is to learn a few names right away and use them during your first class. This lets students see that you are quick and also that you care enough to learn who they are.

Each day, try to learn a few more names. It helps to take attendance out loud for at least a week and require students to raise their hands when called. Through this repetition, you will learn their names.

Realize, however, that you will have times when you forget a student's name. This can occur if a student is very quiet or if a few individuals with similar names sit together in your room. One strategy is to walk around the room passing out papers in the first two weeks of school. Typically, you will want students to retrieve their papers on their own. However, if you are having trouble remembering who a few students are, you can walk around and call out each name as listed on the paper. That way, you can see who reacts.

Checklists for Success

As explained in this and other chapters, much of teaching is confidence. And organization can be a big boon to anyone's confidence. It may help you to use the following lists to help organize yourself before and during the school year. You can also find more comprehensive beginning-of-the-year and end-of-the-year checklists on the CD included with this book.

In Your Room

You will spend a lot of time in your classroom, so make sure that you have created a warm and welcoming environment there. Use the following checklist to make sure your room is ready for your students:

✓ Create bulletin boards with an eye toward enhancing your curriculum. Make sure they are not a distraction to your students.

The Everything N

✓ Organize your room into separate areas devoted to
resources. For example, you might have an area de
work, one for text checkouts, one for learning statior

✓ Place items where they make the most sense in term
words, put your most used files in the cabinet closest

✓ Gather your supplies in specific locations. Make su ....tory
what you have so that you can keep track of your resources.

✓ Clean your desks before the students arrive. You will often come to
school to find dirty desks that have not been cleaned all summer.

✓ Depending on the grade you teach, make sure you have a pencil
sharpener, chalk, erasers, markers, scissors, and crayons.

On Your Desk

You will spend a lot of time at your desk over the next year, so take some
time now to organize your personal space. Following is a list of items that
you should make sure to have at or near your desk for quick reference:

✓ Your course texts and books
✓ Your lesson plan book
✓ Your attendance book and sheets
✓ Hall passes and discipline referrals
✓ The substitute folder and information
✓ Post-it notes, paper clips, paper, pens, and pencils
✓ A stapler, tape, and a pair of scissors

ALERT

Make sure that you follow the correct procedure for reporting any
damage or other problems to your room. Try to take care of any issues
during planning week so you can start the year off right.

In Your Lessons

Finally, you should make sure that when you create lessons, you consider the following:

✓ Learning styles
✓ Multiple intelligences
✓ Varying instruction
✓ Standards
✓ Time to complete
✓ Time to grade
✓ Your goals
✓ Your expectations

While it can seem overwhelming, just take it one step at a time. Realize that you will have lessons that will flop and lessons that will soar. Keep the best, and rework the worst for next year's students. Only through trial and error can you truly become an effective teacher.

CHAPTER 25

Can You Really Do It All?

As a teacher, you will feel that you are being pulled in many directions. You will often be admired, pitied, and derided at the same time. You will find that everyone has expectations of what you should do and how you should teach. This can become overwhelming. However, what really matters is whether you feel good about the job you have done at the end of each day.

A Part of Your Community

Your school is a part of your community, and there are a lot of expectations that the community places upon its teachers. Citizens expect teachers to provide students with an education that prepares them for the future. They look to schools to teach students appropriate behavior. They also expect teachers to ensure that all students learn the basics that will help them function in civic society.

ESSENTIAL

People who look professional will be taken seriously and demand respect. Dress and act like a professional from day one. Though it may sometimes be a pain to get dressed up and make yourself look presentable, realize that the effort will make a difference.

Preparation for Work

Employers today cite the lack of basic skills as the source of many problems with their new employees. Many community leaders feel that schools are not doing enough to prepare students for work. This does not mean that high school students should be learning specific skills, such as running a cash register. What it does mean is that students are expected to leave school with the ability to read and write, perform basic mathematic calculations, and think critically. Knowing how to learn and where to find information is more valuable than being able to recite a list of memorized facts.

Good Citizenship

Communities also expect schools to turn out good citizens. This means they expect you, as a teacher, to reinforce skills such as punctuality and honesty. Some community leaders also stress the importance of teaching students pride in their country and a desire to get involved. The move toward greater community service reflects the growing concern that students should learn to care for their neighbors.

Many schools are actually requiring community service in order for students to graduate. Further, many clubs and organizations require students to participate in and complete service projects. Finally, some scholarships even require students to show that they have volunteered or otherwise helped out their community in substantial ways.

What Parents Want

Parents have many expectations for teachers, some of which are appropriate and some not. Parents should and do expect teachers to provide a quality education to their children. They also expect that you, as the teacher, will treat their children fairly and with dignity. Many parents wish to be involved or at the very least informed of their child's progress.

ALERT

Every once in a while you will deal with parents who deny that their child's actions deserve punishment, even when they have done something completely inappropriate. Realize that you will not be able to change their minds. But do not let this cause you to back off justified punishment.

A Valuable Education

Parents expect that their children will receive a worthwhile education. Most feel that their children are learning valuable information every day. With the increase in high-stakes testing, parents also expect that the educational system will prepare them to pass these exams. When the press highlights students who do not know basic facts, such as the name of the first president of the United States, this harms educators and the state of education.

Respect and Consideration

Parents also expect teachers to respect and care for their children. Every person should be treated with respect and dignity. When teachers do not follow this principle, they set a bad example for their students and they bring down the reputation of the school. It is very difficult to learn in a hostile environment; yet these are all too common.

Remember when you next look out over the children in your room that all of them have a parent or guardian who loves them. Remember to treat them as you would if their parents were actually sitting right next to them. This can help you become more considerate of your students and their needs.

Being Informed

Parents expect to be informed, and appreciate it, when their children are struggling. The younger the student, the more parents expect to be kept informed. Do your best to avoid a situation in which a student is set to fail or not graduate without having discussed it with his parents. Remember, parents can be your best allies in getting students motivated. Parents who feel as though you have shirked your duty of informing them about important situations can cause real problems for you with your administration and district.

As stated previously, you should attempt to call your students and their parents often. Of course, some students require more attention than others. If nothing else, make sure that you contact the parents of these high-need students so that you can get them to help you create a positive educational experience for their children.

Inappropriate Parental Expectations

Most parents believe that education is very important to their children's future life. However, there are some parents who believe that teachers should take over raising their children. They take the attitude that while their children are at school, they are the school's problem. Further, these parents see education as separate from home life. They believe that the entire responsibility for teaching their children falls on the teacher.

The fact is that students whose parents are involved in their education have a greater chance of succeeding, but there is not much you, as a teacher, can do to alter parental expectations. The important thing is to set boundaries for yourself and do the best you can.

Working with Your Students

Students also have major expectations concerning you and their class. They expect you to be in control at all times, and to be fair and consistent. They also expect that what you will be teaching is pertinent to their lives. Make sure that you strive to live up to your students' expectations as much as possible.

Fairness and Consistency

As discussed in Chapter 2, fairness and consistency are two of the most important ingredients to being an effective teacher. When students perceive you as unfair, they will be less likely to listen and less likely to succeed. Remember, students watch every move you make, and they are very perceptive at picking up your prejudices. Make a concerted effort to be fair among all students and consistent from day to day.

Fairness and consistency might be two different terms, but they go hand in hand while teaching. To be fair means to take each person into equal consideration. To be consistent means to treat students the same at all times. One cannot truly exist without the other.

Keeping It Real

Education is about preparing students for their future. You will find that your students will be the most engaged when they feel intimately affected by the information you present. Therefore, you should give some thought to explaining the significance and importance of each of the lessons you complete in class.

This does not mean that you should throw out all lessons that are not going to have direct bearings on your students' lives. Instead, it means that you need to make the connections for your students, especially if they are not obvious. These connections can make a huge difference in student learning.

Appeasing the Administration

Your school's administration will have expectations for you as an employee and as a school ambassador to the community. Administrators will expect you to be a team player and professional at all times. If they believe that you have acted inappropriately, they will discuss this with you and possibly subject you to disciplinary action.

The administration will also expect you to keep your students under control. It is a fact that the teacher who gets a lot of parent and student complaints to administration will be seen as a poor teacher. Unfortunately, in some schools if you write too many discipline referrals, you will be regarded as a person who lacks good classroom management skills. Because referrals are the highest level of punishment you can dole out, they should be used wisely. Make sure to be consistent and fair with discipline, and you will have fewer problems.

Administrators expect you to vary your instruction and make changes and adjustments for students with disabilities. They take IEPs very seriously (as they should) and expect you to make every effort to follow through on each modification. Further, they expect that you will accept all students in your class equally, no matter what their disability.

ESSENTIAL

It is not a good idea, especially as a new teacher, to speak badly of your school to the press or to parents. These types of comments can sometimes undermine the effective education of other teachers at your school. Very vocal teachers will be frowned upon. You must decide which battles you feel are important enough to fight outside the system.

Finally, administration expects you to follow the employee guidelines. As a teacher, you will probably be held to high ethical standards. Whether you wish to believe it or not, your actions both inside and outside the school reflect on the school and all teachers. Therefore, think about the consequences before you act. You will also be required to follow correct procedure for daily tasks. Teachers who try to bend the rules usually end up getting in trouble with their administration.

Setting Your Own Expectations

You will feel pressure to live up to everyone's expectations. However, they are not as important as setting and meeting expectations of your own. Many of your expectations should be the same as those of the community, parents, students, and the administration. However, you do not have to strive to meet those expectations you think are inappropriate for your situation.

Daily Goals

Each evening before you go to sleep or each morning when you wake up, write down a goal or two for the day. Your goals should be challenging, but they should also be very specific and realistic. For example, you might set a goal of getting a student who never speaks up during a class discussion to become involved. Or you might make a goal that you will begin class on time each period. The point of this exercise is that if you have goals, you have something to strive for. Your goals should be compatible with your expectations for yourself and your students. As you complete each goal, cross it off the list and celebrate!

Reach Higher

Never settle for a mediocre performance. Strive to be the teacher who someone will thank someday for truly and positively affecting her life. Strive to be the teacher who helps light a spark for some students who have never enjoyed school in the past. In other words, set your expectations high. When you meet them, raise the bar.

Still, make sure that you are not trying to accomplish the impossible. Remember that your students have minds of their own. You can teach and do your job, but you cannot change a student's personality or conduct. Therefore, your goals should not center upon someone else's behavior. For example, you should not have a goal that "Johnnie will stop pushing Laura today." Make them very personal, and keep the list with you all day long to remind you of your focus.

Opportunities for Growth

You should also stay aware of opportunities for growth. You will most likely be required to perform some sort of professional development every year in order to get recertified. Choose activities and in-service programs that will truly help you develop as a teacher. Attend conferences and listen to others teaching your subjects to find fresh ideas and insights. When you spend time with motivated people, you will find yourself becoming more motivated too.

A few words need to be said about in-service programs and conferences. Sometimes, you will find them to be extremely interesting and worthwhile. Other times, you will find them to be boring and not really worth your time. However, you are a professional, so make sure that you act like one at all times. No matter what, you should respect the person who is leading the in-service program or speaking at the conference. Unfortunately, teachers often make the worst students. You know how you feel when students do not listen and instead talk among themselves in your classroom. Do not be that type of "student."

Many teachers have found that the steps to become nationally certified have proved to be a real growth opportunity to their career. Take some time to look into it. Not only do many states provide monetary incentives for successfully completing this great program, but you will also reap other more intangible benefits. You will learn more about yourself as a teacher as you take a critical look at your practices.

FACT

States across the nation are providing subsidies and incentives for national board certification. Some states provide the same incentive to all teachers. Other states allow individual districts to award their teachers with significant monetary bonuses. However, budget cuts and recent economic woes have caused some states to cut monetary compensation for national board-certified teachers.

You are teaching students with the hope that they will become lifelong learners. However, you must look at yourself to see if you are a good role model for your students. Are you a lifelong learner? Are you someone who enjoys reading about and learning new things? Or are you someone who goes home and turns on the television to while away the hours? Your love of learning will show through to your children, your fellow workers, and your students.

You also may find that when you begin taking on a leadership role in your school, you will grow more as a teacher and a person. Followers allow things to happen to them. They often complain but rarely do anything productive to institute change. Good leaders, on the other hand, should be a source of strength and a proponent for necessary change. They spend time looking for solutions.

You do not have to be an administrator to be a leader. You can choose to lead through your classroom, through positions like team leading, serving as a department head, or chairing a committee. You can simply choose to lead through your attitude. If you are a tactful, positive, motivated hard worker, you can make a difference in your students' lives and in your school.

A Rewarding Career

Teaching is truly a rewarding career. Teachers are special people who choose their life's work not for monetary gain or because it's easy, but because they are called to teach. In the United States, we are very privileged to provide our children with a free appropriate education. Truly effective teachers treat each student as if they have paid handsomely for their education and should get something worthwhile out of it.

It can often be hard, however, to find joy in the job of teaching. Sometimes days are filled with red tape and disruptions. Some students and parents will not respect you no matter what you do. People will make comments to you about how horrible it must be to be a teacher. Yet through it all, remember why you became a teacher: to positively affect the lives of children.

Celebrate Small Victories

Teachers need frequent celebrations. Every time you accomplish a written or unwritten goal is a cause for celebration. Take the time to truly enjoy your small victories. Treasure any words or notes of praise and pull them out when you need a pick-me-up. Spend time with fellow teachers discussing positive comments that you have heard students make. In the end, life on earth is so short that we must grab a hold of every moment and live life to the fullest. If you are spending all week just counting the days to the weekend, then you are not in the right job.

Look on the Bright Side

Much of being happy in life is looking at the positives and working to eliminate the negatives. If you want students and people to like you, be positive in attitude and action. Do not look for trouble, because you will surely find it. Instead, look for inspiration, beauty, humor, and growth in yourself, your students, and your coworkers. Do not spend time focusing on the negatives of teaching. Instead, stay true to your beliefs about the value of people and of education.

ESSENTIAL

Teaching should be fun, interesting, and challenging. It should provide you with many opportunities to grow. To be a happier teacher, celebrate the little things. Remember to measure rewards by single events. You will be happier in the long run.

The Noble Profession

Teaching truly is a noble profession—ever-changing and always challenging. Know that you can meet the challenges of teaching and succeed. It is an amazing thing when students come back to you after they have left your course and tell you how much you have meant to them. As Carl Jung said, "One looks back with appreciation to the brilliant teachers, but with gratitude to those who touched our human feelings. The curriculum is so much necessary raw material, but warmth is the vital element for the growing plant and for the soul of the child."

APPENDIX A

Additional Resources

Further Readings

Brandvik, Mary Lou. *English Teacher's Survival Guide: Ready-to-Use Techniques and Materials for Grades 7–12.* (San Francisco, CA: Jossey–Bass, 1994).

Canter, Lee, and Marlene Canter. *Lee Canter's Assertive Discipline: Positive Behavior Management for Today's Classroom.* (Santa Monica, CA: Lee Canter & Assoc., 1997).

Culham, Ruth. *6 + 1 Traits of Writing: The Complete Guide.* (Jefferson City, MO: Scholastic Paperbacks, 2003).

Gardner, Howard. *Intelligence Reframed: Multiple Intelligences for the 21st Century.* (New York, NY: Basic Books, 2000).

Johnson, Spencer. *Who Moved My Cheese? An Amazing Way to Deal with Change in Your Work and in Your Life.* (New York, NY: Putnam Publishing Group, 1998).

Loewen, James. *Lies My Teacher Told Me: Everything Your American History Textbook Got Wrong.* (New York, NY: Touchstone Books, 2007).

Morgenstern, Julie. *Organizing from the Inside Out, 2nd Edition.* (New York, NY: Henry Holt, 2004).

Ravitch, Diane. *The Language Police: How Pressure Groups Restrict What Students Learn.* (New York, NY: Knopf, 2003).

Sousa, David A. *How the Brain Learns, 2nd Edition.* (Thousand Oaks, CA: Corwin Press, 2000).

Winebrenner, Susan. *Teaching Gifted Kids in the Regular Classroom: Strategies and Techniques Every Teacher Can Use to Meet the Needs of the Gifted and Talented.* (Minneapolis, MN: Free Spirit Publishing, 2000).

Organizations

American Federation of Teachers

The AFT is a teacher's union associated with the AFL–CIO. Among other resources, it provides educators with support and legal aid. It also lobbies congressional leaders concerning educational issues.

🖱 *www.aft.org*

American Library Association

The ALA is the oldest and largest library association in the world. Members include librarians from the public sector, universities, and schools across the nation and the world.

🖱 *www.ala.org*

ASCD (formerly the Association for Supervision and Curriculum Development)

According to their website, ASCD represents "all aspects of effective teaching and learning." While focused more upon administrators and professional development, there is much pertinent information here.

🖱 *www.ascd.org*

Council for Exceptional Children

This organization is dedicated to improving the education provided to gifted students and those with disabilities and varying exceptionalities.

🖱 *www.cec.sped.org/ab*

International Reading Association

The International Reading Association is dedicated to promoting literacy for all students and individuals.

🖱 *www.reading.org*

National Council of Teachers of English

This organization helps bring together English and language arts teachers and provides them with information, resources, and more.

🖱 *www.ncte.org*

National Council of Teachers of Mathematics

This council provides educators with excellent information and resources pertinent to the world of math.

www.nctm.org

National Council for the Social Studies

Find out the latest news for social studies teachers, including standards and more.

www.ncss.org

National Education Association

The NEA is a teacher's union that traces its roots to 1857. The group does many things, including lobbying congressional leaders concerning educational issues and providing legal support for educators.

www.nea.org

National Science Teachers Association

This organization allows science teachers to investigate the latest educational and scientific developments.

www.nsta.org

United States Distance Learning Association

This association provides information, advocacy, and opportunities for distance-learning educators.

www.usdla.org

Online Resources

About.com Elementary Education

An About.com site providing excellent lesson plans, resources, and information for elementary school (K–6) educators.

🖰 *http://k6educators.about.com*

About.com Secondary Education

This site, run by the author of this book, provides lesson plans, resources, information on educational issues, advice, chats, and discussions for secondary school (6–12) educators.

🖰 *http://712educators.about.com*

About.com Private Schools

This site focuses on issues specific to private schools. It is an excellent resource if you plan on teaching in this environment and includes lesson plans, resources, and information.

🖰 *http://privateschool.about.com*

B. F. Skinner Foundation

Learn more about operant conditioning and positive/negative reinforcement at this interesting website.

🖰 *www.bfskinner.org*

Education Week

Read the latest daily and weekly news from *Education Week*. You can sign up for free access.

🖰 *www.edweek.org*

Education World

Another great site for teachers. Find lesson plans, information on professional development, educational news, and an area devoted specifically to administration.

🖰 *www.education-world.com*

ERIC Clearinghouse on Disabilities and Gifted Education

The Educational Resources Information Center (ERIC) provides a wealth of information for teaching gifted students and those with disabilities.

🖱 *www.eric.ed.gov*

Florida Virtual School

The website for the Florida Virtual School, an organization that was discussed in depth in Chapter 22.

🖱 *www.flvs.net*

National Center for Education Statistics

Learn more about the latest statistics collected about education across the United States.

🖱 *http://nces.ed.gov*

U.S. Department of Education

Learn about the latest policies and initiatives affecting the nation's classrooms.

🖱 *www.ed.gov*

State Departments of Education

Alabama: *www.alsde.edu*
Alaska: *www.eed.state.ak.us*
Arizona: *www.ade.state.az.us*
Arkansas: *http://arkansased.org*
California: *www.cde.ca.gov*
Colorado: *www.cde.state.co.us*
Connecticut: *www.state.ct.us/sde*
Delaware: *www.doe.state.de.us*
District of Columbia: *www.k12.dc.us*
Florida: *www.fldoe.org*
Georgia: *www.doe.k12.ga.us*
Hawaii: *http://doe.k12.hi.us*
Idaho: *www.sde.idaho.gov*
Illinois: *www.isbe.state.il.us*
Indiana: *http://ideanet.doe.state.in.us*
Iowa: *www.iowa.gov/educate*
Kansas: *www.ksde.org*
Kentucky: *www.kde.state.ky.us*
Louisiana: *www.doe.state.la.us/lde/index.html*
Maine: *www.state.me.us/education*
Maryland: *www.msde.state.md.us*
Massachusetts: *www.doe.mass.edu*
Michigan: *www.michigan.gov/mde*
Minnesota: *http://education.state.mn.us*
Mississippi: *www.mde.k12.ms.us*
Missouri: *http://dese.mo.gov*

Montana: *www.opi.state.mt.us/index.html*
Nebraska: *www.nde.state.ne.us*
Nevada: *www.doe.nv.gov*
New Hampshire: *www.ed.state.nh.us*
New Jersey: *www.state.nj.us/education*
New Mexico: *www.sde.state.nm.us*
New York: *www.nysed.gov*
North Carolina: *www.dpi.state.nc.us*
North Dakota: *www.dpi.state.nd.us*
Ohio: *www.ode.state.oh.us*
Oklahoma: *www.sde.state.ok.us*
Oregon: *www.ode.state.or.us*
Pennsylvania: *www.pde.state.pa.us*
Rhode Island: *www.ride.ri.gov*
South Carolina: *www.sde.state.sc.us*
South Dakota: *http://doe.sd.gov*
Tennessee: *www.state.tn.us/education*
Texas: *www.tea.state.tx.us*
Utah: *www.usoe.k12.ut.us*
Vermont: *www.state.vt.us/educ*
Virginia: *www.pen.k12.va.us*
Washington: *www.sbe.wa.gov*
West Virginia: *http://wvde.state.wv.us*
Wisconsin: *www.dpi.state.wi.us*
Wyoming: *www.k12.wy.us*

Glossary of Terms and Acronyms

Active listening:
A learned skill enabling you to fully listen and respond to others in the most effective manner possible.

ADA:
American with Disabilities Act. This act prohibits discrimination based on disability.

ADD/ADHD:
Attention deficit disorder/attention deficit hyperactive disorder. ADD/ADHD is a treatable medical condition that results in a combination of distractibility and impulsivity, and hyperactive behavior.

Advanced Placement:
A program run by the College Board whereby high school students complete a rigorous course of study and are then tested on their knowledge. Many colleges award credit to students for passing scores.

Advocate:
An individual working for parents of students with disabilities to ensure their child receives an appropriate education.

Block schedule:
A system whereby a school restructures the school day or week so that students have fewer classes for longer stretches of time.

Bloom, Benjamin:
American educator who developed a hierarchical set of learning objectives known today as Bloom's taxonomy.

Bloom's taxonomy:
A system created by Benjamin Bloom that determines the level of abstraction of common educational questions. The six levels of Bloom's taxonomy in increasing order are: knowledge, comprehension, application, analysis, synthesis, and evaluation.

Bodily kinesthetic intelligence:
The ability to control one's body and skillfully handle objects.

***Brown v. Board of Education*:**
Case tried before U.S. Supreme Court in 1954. The Court decided that "separate educational facilities are inherently unequal." Thus began the era of desegregation of schools.

Busing:
A transportation solution implemented to institute the changes brought about by desegregation. Students are bused from neighborhood schools in an effort to level racial percentages in a district.

Charter schools:
Special public schools that have specific missions and goals, not subject to many of the regulations that traditional public schools must follow. They are generally awarded a charter for a certain number of years with opportunities for renewal.

Co-teaching:
A system in which two certified teachers teach in a room at the same time. This is typically used to accommodate the needs of students with disabilities within the mainstreamed classroom.

Criterion-referenced test:
A test in which questions are written according to specific predetermined criteria. A student knows what the standards are for passing and only competes against himself.

Critical thinking:
Thinking in ways that draws conclusions and makes analyses using facts and information. This type of thinking is typically associated with the upper level of Bloom's taxonomy.

Distance learning:
Education that is received at a geographical location separate from that of the educational institution providing the curriculum and material.

Double sessions:
A situation that typically occurs when schools are overcrowded. The student body is divided and half of the students attend classes in the morning, and the other half attends them in the afternoon or evening.

ESL:
English as a second language. ESL courses teach English and sometimes other subjects to individuals who either grew up speaking no English or who grew up in a home where English was not the primary language.

Existential intelligence:
The ability and desire to ask and search for answers to questions concerning human existence.

FAPE:
Free and Appropriate Public Education. All students are guaranteed FAPE; IDEA was created to ensure that FAPE is available to special-needs or exceptional students.

4×4 plan:
A system whereby a school reorganizes its class time and structure so that students only have four courses per semester, and courses are completed in half the "normal" time.

Full inclusion:
The idea that a student with a disability should be placed in a classroom with nondisabled classmates and should only be removed from the regular classroom if the disability is so severe that even with extra aid and help, the student cannot learn in that environment.

Gardner, Howard:
A leading developmental psychologist who devised the influential theory of multiple intelligences.

Gifted:
A term used by schools to define students who have a high intelligence quotient (IQ) score—usually two standard deviations above the norm—and show other signs of being more advanced than their peers.

High-stakes testing:
A practice that relates success on a standardized test to rewards of one kind or another.

Holistic grading:
A method of grading that has teachers grade in a more intuitive manner. Generally, a group of teachers get together, decide on criteria for grading, and then quickly grade a set of papers based on these criteria.

IDEA:
Individuals with Disabilities Education Act. This act requires that students who have disabilities acquire the same level of education as students without disabilities. The main tool for implementing IDEA is the IEP.

IEP:
Individualized education plan. This is an accountability measure that must be followed by the school, special education teachers, and regular education teachers. If accommodations are not made according to the IEP, the school can be liable for disciplinary and legal actions.

Interpersonal intelligence:
Ability to relate well with others and to respond appropriately.

Intrapersonal intelligence:
Having a strong sense of self-awareness and the ability to understand one's own feelings, values, and beliefs.

LD:
Learning disabled. Individuals with learning disabilities often have difficulty interpreting what they see and/or hear or have problems linking information from different parts of the brain.

Learning communities:
A system that places students into "schools within schools" based on their abilities or career goals.

Learning styles:
Different approaches to learning. There are three major types of learners: visual, auditory, and tactile/kinesthetic. Each person has a learning style by which she learns the best.

Linguistic intelligence:
Having well-developed verbal skills and the ability to recognize the difference between sounds and rhythms of speech.

Logical-mathematical intelligence:
The ability to see patterns and think in logical sequences.

LRE:
Least restrictive environment. The idea of LRE has emerged from the belief that a student with a disability should be placed in a classroom with nondisabled classmates and should only be removed from the regular classroom if the disability is so severe that even with extra aid and help, the student cannot learn in that environment.

Magnet schools:
Special schools that focus on a specific interest and use different types of organization for students with similar interests. For example,

a performing arts magnet school offers and requires more performing arts courses than are available in a traditional school.

Multiple intelligences:
A theory devised by Howard Gardner, which proposes that the traditional intelligence quotient (IQ) measure of intelligence does not show the whole or even part of the picture. Instead, there are eight multiple intelligences and each person has his own strengths and weaknesses: linguistic, logical-mathematical, spatial, bodily kinesthetic, musical, interpersonal, intrapersonal, and naturalist. Recently, Gardner added a ninth intelligence—existential intelligence.

Musical intelligence:
The ability to recognize musical patterns and discern rhythm and pitch.

Naturalist intelligence:
A strong affinity with nature and ability to classify plants, animals, and other natural objects.

Online learning:
Education that is delivered through the Internet. The Florida Virtual School is one example of an online learning school.

Operant conditioning:
A system of discipline and behavior modification whereby an association is created between an action and a consequence.

National certification:
A rigorous program in which teachers create a portfolio and take an exam in order to become nationally certified.

Negative reinforcement:
Combining punishment with positive experiences for correct behavior.

No Child Left Behind Act of 2001:
This act, signed into law by President George W. Bush, has the goal of reducing the achievement gap between disabled and minority students and those who are traditionally successful in the classroom environment.

Norm-referenced test:
A test that determines a student's placement on a normal distribution curve. On this type of assessment, students compete against each other.

Paradigm:
A community's shared set of assumptions, values, and practices that shapes their reality. When major changes occur in education and life, it is sometimes said that a paradigm has shifted.

Pedagogy:
The profession of teaching.

Portfolio:
A collection of a student's work used to help determine progress and grade.

Positive reinforcement:
Praising and rewarding students for correct behavior.

Reliability:
In terms of assessments, a test is considered reliable if it allows for stable estimates of student ability. In other words, it achieves similar results for students who have similar ability and knowledge levels.

Rubric:
A grading tool that defines the requirements each part of an assignment must meet to receive full or partial credit.

Senior project:
Typically, a portfolio or project created during a student's senior year in high school.

Scaffolding:
Providing students with a basic structure from which they are to complete their work. This is done for students who need some help framing their work. The eventual goal is to "remove" the scaffold altogether.

Sick building:
A building where people become sick as a result of poor air circulation and design.

Social promotion:
The practice of promoting students to the next grade even though their progress does not merit such promotion.

Skinner, B. F.:
The psychologist who studied reinforcement and operant conditioning; his studies led to the development of programmed instruction.

CD Table of Contents

Beginning of the Year Checklist

End of the Year Checklist

Seating Chart Examples (4)

Student Information Sheet

Classroom Check In/Check Out Sheet

Substitute Information Form

Sample Substitute Lesson Plan

Blank Substitute Lesson Plan

Sample Emergency Lesson Plan

Blank Emergency Lesson Plan

Parent Contact Log

Parent Conference Form

Blank Weekly Lesson Plan Form

Blank Daily Lesson Plan Form

Sample Unit Plan

Blank Unit Plan Form

Blank Monthly Calendar

Blank Weekly Calendar

Sample Middle Grades Welcome Letter

Sample High School Syllabus

Sample Elementary Classroom Rules

Teacher Celebrations List

Graphic Organizers

Sample Double Venn Diagram

Blank Double Venn Diagram

Sample Triple Venn Diagram

Blank Triple Venn Diagram

Sample Series of Events Chain Diagram

Blank Series of Events Chain Diagram

Sample Problem/Solution Outline

Blank Problem/Solution Outline

Sample Semantic Map

Blank Semantic Map

Index